Living Guilt Free

Reflections on Love, Healing, and the Art of Forgiveness

NAOMI SCHVARTZ-COHEN

Producer & International Distributor
eBookPro Publishing
www.ebook-pro.com

LIVING GUILT FREE

NAOMI SCHVARTZ-COHEN

Translation: Seree Zohar
Editing: Nancy Alroy

Contact: naomiwsw@gmail.com

ISBN 9789655755978

Dedication

I dedicate this book to my parents,
Hana and Hillel, our angels up in heaven.

To my children, Liat, Erez, Alon, Lior,
and to the children of my heart,
David, Shirly, and Sahrit.

To my grandchildren, Tom, Taylor, Yali,
Ben, Itai, Ella, Eitan, Matan, Gal, and Maya –
you are all the pillars of my life.

Chapter 1

Tuesday rolled up.

Eva parked in the lot facing the city's neighborhood community center. Switching the ignition off, she stayed in her seat, glanced at the dashboard clock, then at her wristwatch, a Rado that her husband had gifted to her some years earlier. Eva had spied the elegant timepiece in a Swiss window display when they were still much younger. "One day," she'd grinned, pointing to it, "when we're rich, that's the watch I want." He remembered.

An hour to go. This would be the first meeting of a year-long course that her therapist had recommended, with the intent of possibly bringing new insights into her life after the crisis she experienced two years prior.

Classical music played softly in the car: Beethoven's 5th, which matched the mood of her stormy thoughts and heartbeat. Her breathing quickened; her thoughts jumbled like a whirlwind.

Glancing around, she noted that the nearby shops were bustling with boisterous kids and parents. Here and there, an older person with a caregiver would shuffle up and rest on a bench for a few minutes. In the small park nearby, birds chirped in the treetops. Lives were carrying on just as they should.

Heralding dusk, Eva's favorite time of day, the sky began darkening.

Her thoughts blurred. She felt as though she was in some kind of imaginary visualization that wasn't truly real. Her watch showed the passage of time which, just moments earlier, had seemed so clear.

A bird's fluttering wings reminded her of first coffees at home when life was uncomplicated and logical. That is, until everything went topsy turvy one Friday two years ago.

When asked on occasion what exactly happened that particular morning, she was surprised to discover that she had no logical answer. It was nothing more than a sensation, an inner voice, prodding her.

More than a decade earlier, she and her husband had decided to drop back to a five-day work week: Sundays to Thursdays, and spend Fridays together. They would start out at a relaxed pace, giving themselves time for things they hadn't managed to do during the rush of the work week, busy with careers in fields they loved and the needs of their four children. Slowly and steadily, Fridays turned into days where each did things he or she wanted to do in the mornings, separate from one another, only joining forces again at lunchtime, often spent together with the children at a restaurant near their home.

That Friday morning in May, Eva woke and stretched lazily. She'd gone to bed very late: she was a night person, as were all their kids. Three had already flown the coop. The youngest was still home, but often away on military service. Eva already had two grandchildren whose giggles always brought a smile to her face. She could hear them now as they were strapped into the car for the ride to kindergarten. Eva's eldest daughter Lily and her husband lived in a home built on the large plot of land behind Eva's own. How Eva had loved drafting the plans for that house!

The shades were open. Soft natural light filled the spacious bedroom. It had been so easy for her, as an architect, to renovate it. Curtains the color of late-sunset orange dressed the windows. The scent of citrus blooms from trees in the garden wafted in on the early spring breeze. Sprinklers in the neighboring yard where her good friends lived began a soft ch-ch-ch.

Shadow, her loyal dog, barked with joy when the neighbor, who was nuts about her grandchildren, came out to greet them.

Eva's husband was already dressed. On Fridays he often held informal meetings with business contacts. Coming over to her, he kissed her cheek and brought her a cup of steaming hot black coffee. Eva loved that aroma. It always reminded her of when, at eighteen years old, she boarded a Varig Airlines jet on her way to meet relatives in Sao Paulo, Brazil. The sweet memory of that vacation made her smile whenever it popped up in her mind.

"I'm heading out to a business meeting at the company's new offices," her husband said.

"Ah, great!" Eva responded warmly. "Can you take some shots of the ground floor? Last week I was sent a proposal to plan a café in that space. I'm supposed to have a meeting there in a few days."

Before his meetings, her husband usually popped over to the local bakery, returning with fresh pastries. Eva stepped into the shower, also renovated some years earlier. The bathroom was roomy, well-lit, tiled in dark burgundy and outfitted with a glossy white closet boasting unique handles sculpted in the image of a man and a woman. The huge wall mirror was hooked up with special lighting for makeup, not that Eva was big on makeup. She nodded at her reflection: maybe the day would come when she'd make more use of that mirror.

Dressing for her regular Friday morning class at the gym, another structure she had planned on one floor of the building where her parents lived, Eva confirmed that she'd be meeting Lily later for a bout of shopping.

Eva wasn't nearly as into working out at the gym as her husband, a dedicated sportsman, but she'd realized it was time to adopt some new habits.

She heard her husband come back but, this time, he didn't put the pastries down on the table and leave. Instead, he came upstairs to the mezzanine-level bedroom of the expansive home Eva had designed early in their married lives, some twenty-six years ago.

"In the end, the meeting's taking place in the company's main building. Sorry, but I won't be able to take those pix," he said softly.

In that flash of an instant, everything switched gears.

She knew, but how could she?

Or perhaps it began two months earlier.

Through one of the companies connected to her husband's business, the couple was invited to a three-day event in Florence. It was a huge annual gala, this time with an appearance by the Israel Philharmonic Orchestra, specially flown in. Florence was a gorgeous place, one Eva never tired of visiting. Every stone, every building in that city held snippets of history, stunning Renaissance architecture from the city's most prolific period of development under the Medici family's patronage. Florence's landscape included luxurious palaces and unusual bridges over the Arno River. Every other street corner held a charming café, and streets crisscrossed via picturesque plazas adorned with fountains. Like so many old cities in Italy, Florence conveyed romance, pomp and splendor.

Those three days were blessed with pleasant sunshine. In the mornings, while her husband was at business meetings, she wandered the museums, stopped to gaze at buildings, breathed in the old-style atmosphere, and indulged in the gelato she loved, happy to forego lunch at the hotel for her a pistachio ice cream.

But something was niggling at the back of her mind. Every

time she stepped out from their hotel room, she found her husband on his cellphone. If she asked who was on the line, he'd simply say "business call." She found that a little odd, since the company's managers and senior staffers were all staying at their hotel.

Eva didn't normally accompany her husband on these professional conferences, and he would frequently tell her how much he appreciated her for not imposing like so many of the other wives who's presence 'disrupted the professional mingling,' as he defined it. In fact, she was usually busy with her own work projects and couldn't free up time for so many trips abroad. She also felt that a few days' separation here and there would give them each some space, which was healthy for any marriage.

When the event came to a close, they switched to a different hotel for the weekend. It took several hours to get there, passing through the rich colors of vineyards and farms, old stone homes, wooden barns and brick wineries. She could still remember the hotel in the heart of vineyard territory: perfect hospitality, delicious meals, a heated swimming pool surrounded by sculptures and a relaxing garden with cobblestone paths lined by fragrant blossoms.

But the phone calls continued there, too. Eva decided, consciously or unconsciously, to distance the thoughts scratching at her mind. Her husband was her best friend and she loved him dearly. They'd built a wonderful life together.

She recalled a specific conversation with her husband just a few days after their return. It made her smile bitterly. They were standing on the staircase at home. She was on her way down to the home office; he had just come home from his day at work. They were talking about someone who was clearly cheating on his wife.

"Well, we both know that his wife doesn't let the guy go abroad alone," Eva said. "You know, I read that ninety percent of men cheat, but you're in the ten percent that doesn't, I'm sure of that."

"Yeah, she tags along, but you don't need to go abroad to cheat," he said, grinning. Eva nodded. "True," she said, never imagining how that statement would tear her life apart months later.

That Friday morning her husband left the house, the door slamming behind him a little too forcefully. That's uncharacteristic, she thought. And that's when, in a kind of inexplicable lightbulb moment, she decided to do something she could never explain rationally. Stepping out of a quick shower, she called to cancel her gym class, dressed in a blue suit and white blouse, slid behind the steering wheel of her car, and set off for the main building of her husband's company.

Her heart raced. Her head throbbed. Her chest hammered in a weird, scary way. She fiddled with the radio but every sound it emitted hurt her ears. Deep inside herself, she knew she'd arrive at an empty parking lot and a vacant building. She knew this with such certainty that she needed to stop at a gas station to catch her breath, calm down, and buy a coffee and croissant. That's when she remembered she'd left the house without eating.

Reaching the company parking lot, her gaze immediately registered its starkness. She wanted to scream. Instead, she walked to the front door and addressed the security guard.

"My husband's got a meeting here," she said, forcing herself to smile and keep her tone normal. "I need to speak to him."

What the guard saw was an elegantly dressed woman speaking a bit too loudly and on the verge of tears.

"Madam, sorry, but nobody's here."

The tears flowed. "No, you're lying," Eva accused, "my husband's in his office."

"Madam," the guard said, beginning to anger, "if you don't leave the premises, I'll have to call the police."

Sniffling, head lowered, Eva about-faced and returned to her car, the gift that her husband bought for her fiftieth birthday two years ago "because you don't need the Jeep anymore, it's not like you need to chauffeur the kids around anymore," he said as he handed her the keys. There wasn't anything wrong with the new car, but she did love her old high-chassis Jeep. All she wanted, and she had dropped enough hints, was a new laptop.

She slumped in the driver's seat.

It was now conclusive, what she hadn't wanted to see for years. She wept. Someone passing by noticed her and knocked on the window. That startled her.

"You alright?" the man said. "Need help?"

"No. Thanks. I'm okay," she managed to answer. Wiping her eyes, her watch showed that she would now be late. She swiveled the key, fiddled with the radio, found a station playing calm songs of the kind she loved and, taking a deep breath, drove to the mall and parked. She tried to compose herself before going inside.

Scowling, Lily was waiting at the point they'd decided on.

"Mom? What's going on?" Lily's face instantly changed to concern.

"Your father's got a lover," Eva answered. Just like that: without sweetening the pill, without preamble, without thinking about the consequences.

"I know," Lily answered softly. Eva was sure she'd collapse. Her daughter sat her down and quickly brought a glass of water.

"We've suspected it for a while now," Lily said after seeing that Eva was okay. "I didn't say anything because we weren't certain and we didn't want to wake any demons."

Shopping, of course, was off the day's agenda. They didn't have the patience for it. Instead, they wandered around a bit until Eva breathing returned to normally and she knew she wouldn't faint.

Eva decided not to say anything to anyone, yet. For now, Lily was the only one who realized how deeply shaken Eva was. Back at home, Eva went into her bedroom thinking she'd nap for a while. She didn't sleep at all. 'How can I look him in the eye again?' she kept asking herself, especially after she heard him come in the door.

That Friday evening, as they did almost every Friday evening, Eva's parents came to visit. They had a close relationship, as did her parents with their grandchildren and great-grandchildren. Her mother carried in a heavy pot of enticingly aromatic Hungarian goulash, her father brought his warm, loving smile and hugs and, right away, they started to play with the great-grandkids.

Eva's two oldest sons arrived for the family meal along with their girlfriends. The youngest son also walked in, dropping his army rucksack at the entrance with a heavy thud.

The three sons studied their mother for a few moments. Something didn't feel right.

"Mom? Are you alright?" the oldest asked.

"Sure, all good. I think I might have caught a cold," Eva answered as a way of explaining her puffy eyes.

Was her husband ignoring her? That's how it felt to Eva.

The traditional Friday night dinner, ushering in the start of the Sabbath, began with her father making the blessing over the wine. Eva muttered the words along with him, suddenly realizing that these weekly happy family meals may not continue as they had all these years.

She was looking around the house with new eyes now: the beautifully set dinner table, the bouquets that her granddaughter chose and which they arranged together, as they did every week. She looked at the candles that her mother lit and made the ritual blessing over. She glanced at each of her children, her son-in-law, her sons' girlfriends, her husband, her parents, at Shadow the dog waiting patiently next to her Dad as he always did when he saw her father pick up the goblet to sanctify the wine.

After saying 'Amen' in unison, the family sat down to eat. Would this be their last Friday night family get-together, at least, in this format? They'd been enjoying this ritual for the past twenty-six years. It was evident to Eva that, from now on, everything in her life that she had taken for granted would never be the same again.

Now, back in her car, with only ten minutes remaining until the meeting was due to begin, her mind was racing with thoughts and memories, Eva noticed that the sun was setting, staining the sky red, and took off her sunglasses. The phone rang. Eva answered, sounding as though she'd been woken from a reverie.

"Hey, Ev, it's me," her sister said. "I saw your text message. Best of luck."

Eva had told only her children and her sister that she was starting the course that day. Her parents had no clue about any of the recent events: she told them she was going to a business meeting.

Ten minutes until the meeting's start. The feelings she'd recently experienced were surfacing: the fear, the uncertainty, but also anticipation over this next stage in a series that began two years earlier.

Wiping her tears, she picked up her tote. In it was a newly purchased notebook and a gorgeous pink Swarovski pen which her neighbors gave her as a fiftieth birthday gift. Taking a deep breath, she stepped onto the asphalt and headed for the community center.

CHAPTER 2

"Nothing I see in this room [on this street, from this window, in this place] means anything."

Eva entering the local community center and found the room earmarked for chess activities. From the two-story building's broad lobby a staircase led to the upper floor where the course was set to begin. The arrow on a handwritten sign pointed to the elevator but Eva decided to take the stairs. That would allow her another deep breath or two before joining the group. She pushed the door open and noted how ordinary the room was: green linoleum floor showing wear and tear in places, the neon lighting's harsh glow reminiscent of so many supermarkets, and several old-fashioned inset spotlights of the kind she avoided like the plague in her architectural projects because the light they emitted, rather than making a space feel warm, conveyed the atmosphere of an interrogation room.

Eleven upholstered Breuer-style chairs with a folding table extension for writing were arranged in a semi-circle, recalling college classrooms which, no more than a year earlier, she'd decided to leave after two years of Gender and East Asia studies. How she'd looked forward to her studies at the time!

Eva hesitated and eventually sat down. Slowly more chairs began to fill with men and women who'd never met each other before. People glanced at each other, smiled politely, perhaps a little worriedly. She suddenly realized that over the coming year these people would become a significant part of her life. Perhaps they and the group leader would help her open a new door and find a way to forgive.

A pleasant looking man, the facilitator, walked in calmly. Like her father's, his blue eyes radiated tranquility. A striped scarf was wrapped with casual elegance around his neck: clearly a man aware of his image, yet who shies away from making a fashion statement. He seemed about her own age, early fifties.

He sat down and smiled to the group. "Welcome and nice to meet you," he began, "I'm Avraham." He studied each person, his glance moving slowly from one to the next. When is eyes reached hers, which had long since ceased to smile, she found that his gaze was penetrating and something in her changed. It was then that she realized she was indeed in the right place. She felt her body relax. Even the headache she'd had right before arriving began to fade.

As the meeting progressed, she understood that this was Avraham's way of scanning each person's aura to assess their state of mind. As Avraham called out the names of those present, Eva sought an aspect in each of them that would allow her to attach each name to the person and serve as her prompt for the next meeting.

Remembering people's names was a longtime problem for her. To tackle this, in the first meeting for every project she took on, when the engineers and contractors she'd be closely working with for the next few months, were being introduced, she would jot down a comment for herself as a way of associating each name to the person.

"Emily, Odette, Yoli, Manu, Nathan, Sharon, Rachel, David, Tamra, Sarai, Eva." Eva wrote an associative clue down next to each name. Emily: body type similar to her own, lowered eyes. Odette: hair carefully tied back. Nathan: full bodied, sad. Manu: makes a strong impression. Yoli: her mother's name...

"Every week we'll meet and practice the points noted in each chapter of the book, and you'll continue working on these during the week," Avraham explained. "I want you to write down questions and comments and we'll go through them together the next time we meet."

He sat down. "The book is structured around 365 lessons. One a day. The book was received through spirit communication and presented to the world by two psychologists, Dr. William Thetford and Dr. Helen Cohn Schucman, both from Columbia University in New York. It took seven years to publish, was translated into twenty-seven languages, and is being actively employed worldwide."

Avraham halted, locking eyes with each of the group's members before continuing. "I first came across this book thirty years ago. As a psychologist, I realized that a standardized path of therapy where the client sits facing me isn't sufficient. After meeting with Phyllis Schlemmer, one of the women leading 'A Course in Miracles' around the world, I sensed that this was where I could give my clients added value."

"From early childhood I knew I could sense things others couldn't. I could feel things that were far greater than myself. When I spoke about these feelings to others, they were viewed as weird, not dependable. 'Oh, that's just your imagination,' is the kind of phrase I usually heard in response."

Avraham leaned forward a little in his chair. "After doing the course here in Israel, I translated the book with my then partner, Ruth Schick. It took us twelve years. Since then, and parallel to conventional therapy, I've been facilitating this course."

"What we'll go through is not easy. The studies involve not only a good deal of reading, but primarily some complex emotional, mental and intellectual work. The book revolves around several philosophical statements which are not easily digested."

Eva smiled, recalling the philosophy classes she'd taken at university during the half semester when she'd joined students young enough to be her own children. She hadn't understood a word. But as time passed and the scope of materials she read expanded, along with discussions with her own kids, she did progress, discovering the overt and covert messages. Slowly she began reading contemporary philosophical texts from the likes of Jacques Derrida, as well as complex ancient texts by Plato, with whose allegory 'The Cave' she felt a strong link. She, too, had felt she was in a dark cave and that her soul didn't really want to go outside and see what was happening beyond the cave, beyond the realities of her life.

"As part of the process," Avraham resumed, "you'll need to cope with axioms, with questions about the nature of existence as individuals and as units within society. You'll need to break the conventions around knowledge, culture and perhaps even everything you've ever believed in. Questions may come up about your very existence, about the place you perceive yourself to be in relative to others around you, and how that compares to what others reflect to you.

"Sometimes there's a huge disparity in how we perceive reality. Studying this book helps connect and understand physical reality versus metaphysical reality. In other words, you'll examine your sensations and feelings in light of events occurring in your lives. Processes of healing and forgiveness aren't easy and you'll need to be patient, very patient, and perhaps some of you will crack along the way, and that's okay too. There's no single truth, no one path to healing," Avraham emphasized. "Each of us finds our own right way."

Avraham paused. "Those of you who complete the course will be thankful your whole lives and will begin fulfilling your true purpose, the one you were destined for when you arrived in this world."

That made Eva smile. She was skeptical about what she might learn and didn't believe that the process would bring full healing. After two years of intensive therapy, she felt she'd pretty much come to her maximum ability to contain additional changes and surprises in her life. But since Iris, her therapist, who was familiar with Avraham's work, felt that a group therapy framework would help, especially considering the book's message which would influence her positively, Eva signed up. Iris called Avraham 'the miracle worker.' Despite her difficulty in believing she might benefit from the course, she trusted Iris, who knew Eva inside out.

Avraham's description of his childhood experiences fascinated Eva. True, her own profession centered around very materialistic items and structures, but she'd always been curious about something else she felt and couldn't explain in words, something beyond usual sensations, something like Avraham's experiences, which is why Eva often felt that she wanted to help others.

Like her, Avraham had also felt that the academic, logical and rational path was not necessarily the only correct one. These feelings, with her since early childhood, were a boon when she set about planning structures and designing large interiors. They would later contribute when she herself began supporting other women. It was as though someone was leading her, holding her hand and guiding her through a process, providing her with something more, which she couldn't yet put in words.

"In addition to the course and the processes where we'll learn more about each other," Avraham added, "I suggest that every few lessons, when one of you feels that the topic of a lesson really speaks to you, shakes you up inside, we start or end that meeting with that person's personal story."

Something about Avraham's voice captivated Eva. On one hand he spoke forthrightly, sometimes even with a type of truth that wasn't pleasant, but it was definitely a voice that came from knowing, from hearing, from conveying a feeling of tranquility. Occasionally he sat tensely on the edge of his seat;

and other times his posture was super relaxed, leaning on the chair's back as though conveying the chair's voice.

Eva remembered that, frequently enough, entrepreneurs and constructors would say that her tone of voice infused the space with peacefulness, which was interesting in a primarily male field. She would have a feeling that she wasn't sufficiently assertive and yet now, listening to Avraham, she realized that the way to be assertive could also come from a measured yet confident, knowing voice.

Excitement palpably rippled through the group as Avraham handed out copies of the thick volume. A simple action which nonetheless felt ceremonial.

"Before we begin, let's take a short break, and get to know each other a bit," he said, gesturing to the refreshments.

As she always tended to be, Eva was impatient to get started. A quick reader, she sat a short distance from the others and leafed through the book, trying to garner some inkling of its contents. She realized that this time the learning process would be different from those she'd experienced over the past two years. This time it wouldn't be like reading from professional literature, or spiritual texts such as Joseph Murphy's 'The Power of Your Subconscious Mind' or even books by Deepak Chopra and others. Nor would it be like theoretical studies on separation, or how mourning is processed. She recalled how odd it had been to think in those terms when Iris explained what Eva would experience.

Eva was familiar with the five stages of mourning: denial, anger, bargaining, depression, and acceptance. She'd learned about them when volunteering to assist families whose children had fallen in battle after the Second Lebanon War. It dawned on her that she wouldn't be able to skip any of the meetings, no matter how tough continued attendance might be, right when she'd finally begun understanding her life; just as it was impossible to skip a day of one's life, for better or worse. Every moment was part of her soul, and the process that her soul chose for her.

It was time to mingle, she decided, and not sit on the sidelines watching others. That brought to mind the exercise from the sociology course: being in the company of familiar people but watching and listening as though it was the first time you'd met. It was a dynamic which she felt no longer suited her needs.

She noticed Emily gazing out through the window, evidently not wanting to be here, and decided to go over and chat. For some reason Eva felt a connection with Emily, whose eyes were sad, much like Eva's which hadn't smiled for two years now. But Emily was not having it. Perhaps, Eva thought, it's not yet the right time.

Eva moved closer to the group clustered around the refreshments table, smiled, praised the cake which David brought to their first meeting; the regular initial acquaintance questions began: "Where do you live?," "What do you do?," "Married?," "Kids?" and so on, questions that strangers use to position each other. No one knew anyone else. They had come from all over Israel.

Eva realized that for years she hadn't allowed herself to be truly involved in anything aside from being a dedicated mother, and grandmother to her two gorgeous grandchildren. She'd taken on the role of devoted wife, designer, sister, daughter to wonderful parents, career woman. But she'd never given herself the freedom to simply be Eva.

She didn't have friends. Who had time to meet up with friends? In retrospect, she couldn't quite fathom why, in fact, she didn't have 'girls' nights out' at cafés or mornings sharing a fun activity. Why had those had always seemed petty, extraneous, a waste of time? She'd never stopped to think about what she actually wanted. Up to the moment when her life had shattered two years earlier everything seemed to be a continuum:

family, parents, career, trips abroad, affluence. She lacked nothing. Frequently at night she found it hard to fall asleep because something seemed to be missing, but then the morning would come and the previous night's disturbing thoughts would disappear and life would go on as usual.

"Who'd like to be first to share your personal story in one of the upcoming meetings?" Avraham asked at some point.

No one said a word.

In a spontaneous response Eva decided to take the challenge. Why not be first? After the processes she'd already completed, it would be nice to receive advice and be heard. This would be the first time in years that she was willing to talk about herself. She still had no idea where this journey would lead, but she was definitely feeling more secure.

Avraham asked who'd be willing to read out the first, second and third lessons. They filled the first three pages, representing the first three days of the first week.

"These three chapters are the foundation of what we'll learn here," he explained, "which is why we'll relate to them as one lesson."

Nathan read the longish title of the first lesson: "Nothing I see in this room [on this street, from this window, in this place] means anything."

He then continued right on to the title of the second lesson, "I have given everything I see in this room, on this street, from this window, in this place, all the meaning that it has for me."

Eva noted people shifting in their seats at the weighty words, which were affecting her too. If so, it wasn't just a matter of perspective; people anthropomorphize objects, attribute human characteristics or behavior, to match their needs, attaching to them names and symbols and sometimes imbuing them with excessive significance. Eva wondered where this was all going.

Eva watched Avraham. She glanced at the strangers seated in the room. Was she imbuing it with too much significance?

Could she be making a mistake? Suddenly she began comprehending that perhaps, for too long, she'd been handing the reins of her life over to others: her husband, the father of her children; her career; everyone around her. Perhaps her life was a great protective bubble beyond which she couldn't see. And mostly, couldn't see herself. See Eva.

Listening to Nathan's voice as he read, Eva thought he sounded vulnerable. Avraham also caught a change in the emotion and firmness of tone.

"Nathan, does this statement repulse you to your core?"

Tears welled, then spilled down Nathan's cheeks. "The issue is still hard for me to talk about," Nathan said softly, "but I probably will at some point. The second chapter's title certainly touches on my raw sorrow."

Eva understood that what he said was not just true for him, but for her too. She smiled towards him as a way of letting him know that he wasn't alone.

"My friends," Avraham's tone was jocular, "I think flipflops like the ones you're wearing, Eva, should be forbidden on feet like yours." Everyone laughed, Eva included, even though sexist comments of that nature really bothered her. But there was a feeling of release from the tenseness and Eva let it pass without a fuss, happy that after so many years of hiding behind suits meant to impress, someone noticed her feminine side.

After beginning gender studies at university, Eva called herself 'a feminist with red nail polish.' Since then, she made sure there was always a pair of black patent-leather flipflops in her array of footwear.

The laughter settled down and Nathan read the third chapter's title: "I do not understand anything I see in this room [on this street, from this window, in this place]."

Eva noticed beads of sweat showing on some foreheads, as though the group participants had suddenly understood what they'd be going through during the course.

"Despite this statement's complexity," Avraham said, "it provides comfort: we're all human, and we really don't understand everything. The object of these initial lessons is to break our conventions, our preconceptions about the here and now, the truths that we bring into this room. These lessons shatter our beliefs, habits and norms. Only then can we start rebuilding. Only then can we ascertain whether we're truly serving our purpose for our own needs without being dependent on others." He paused. "Not on objects, not on people, and not on the news."

Avraham's name contains his purpose: a spiritual father with a pleasant guiding nature, thought Eva, remembering that he is also a psychologist, which made her instantly relax, since his manner of speech and its content held a lightly academic tone.

Eva had already attained improved spirituality in her life. Since childhood, the unknown had been an attraction: shortwave radio had fascinated her and she'd listen at night, trying to hear what was happening out there, even enjoying the sounds of languages she couldn't understand. She'd lie in bed at night thinking about human mortality. As a young girl she found those thoughts a little disturbing but, over time, she realized that the human soul is infinite and that we came into the world not as a new soul but as a repeatedly assigned reincarnation.

Eva had studied numerous fields aside from architectural design. The broader range of studies enabled her to volunteer for many years in a center for sexually abused women. Despite her own currently difficult experiences, she did not halt her volunteer activities but continued to assist women experiencing critical events. Some women were so harshly affected that the words caught in their throats, so much so that their voices would actually disappear.

Eva's daughter Lily encouraged her to join a serious yoga class. That led to Eva visiting the city of Varanasi in India. Even though she was the oldest in the group, she practiced meditation with Guruji, the guru who mentored Lily's teacher. There, Eva immersed herself in a vastly different lifestyle from her customary abundance and convenience. She was struck by how Indians could live in abject poverty yet smile and be pleasant.

She delved into mindfulness, transcendent communication, healing stones, Reiki. She'd gifted each of her children crystals in velvet pouches when they were still young. Her father often chuckled, claiming she was the reincarnation of his own grandmother, known in Hungary for having natural powers of healing.

Yet on the other hand in her role as an architect planning homes and commercial projects, she felt a close connection with the land, to the physical location of a structure, to lines and knowledge and technology. She was always very present, precise, and committed. She was driven to break the barriers. Could this be the hidden kernel of her approach to being in India?

Eva was ready to devote herself to the course and its process. The time had come to bare the hidden, to feel that moment she'd experienced in the New York Museum of Modern Art standing before a gold-painted mannequin, its eyes marked by two zippers. One zipper was shut. The other was partly... open? Shut? The sculpture had made Eva burst into unstoppable tears. It was a moment of intense comprehension.

That happened on her first trip to America after her husband left their marital home. It was the first time since her flight to Brazil as a lone eighteen year old that she'd traveled on her own. For years she'd loved traveling accompanied: by her husband, her daughter, or other family members. She hadn't been worried about the travel, per se. She traveled frequently. That time, though, it had just felt extremely odd, new.

She was hurting so much that she cried through most of the flight. One of the cabin crew actually noticed and asked if she was alright. "Yes, thanks. I'm just going through some massive life changes and the tears won't stop," Eva answered, trying nonetheless to soften the effect with a wobbly smile. Afterwards she wondered why she shared that with the flight attendant, who nodded. In sympathy? Empathy?

Yes, the time had definitely come to see, clearly.

As the meeting came to a close, Avraham urged them to read several chapters ahead before their next encounter. Doing so would make it possible for them to share feelings roused by specific content, even if others hadn't read that far forward. "Reading ahead connects you to the book, to the miracles waiting for you in your lives, to challenges and modes of thinking. Sharing your reactions also encourages others, who might be wary of the book's content, to continue reading."

That ended the meeting. Pleasant goodbyes were said. Most people hugged each other briefly even though not much had been shared yet. The atmosphere was one of setting out together on a journey without any concept of where it would lead. Eva felt a special, inexplicable connection to Nathan. She also felt somewhat connected to Emily: even though they hadn't conversed, Eva sensed that she'd enjoy being in her company. She knew she'd never forget Yoli's name.

What had brought the others to this year-long course, which was no simple commitment she realized, especially after she'd listened to Avraham? She wondered about that as she crossed the parking lot to her car and slid behind the wheel of her recently purchased Jeep, a gift to herself simply because she liked that kind of car.

"If you're replacing the old with the new, then all the way!" her daughter-in-law had suggested. Eva took it on board.

She pulled into her driveway. For some months now the second car it was built for hadn't been there, a sign of what was happening in her life. But she loved that home, which was so full of light. She spied a light on in the kitchen and heard Shadow's barks of joy. Eva unlocked the front door. Shadow was all over her in an instant. Of course a dog that was blacker than black would be named that, especially since her youngest had found the pup in the garbage dump, filthy black, some fourteen years ago.

He had been on his way to a friend up the street when he heard the cries of tiny pups. Retrieving them both, he took them home and put them on a towel in a box. They curled up and fell asleep. At the time the family had a female terrier called Shade, who immediately stepped into the role of mother. Eva's son found a home for one of the two pups with the ice-cream-truck man whose rounds took him to their street once a week. For five years, until she died of old age, Shade watched over the remaining pup.

At least someone in this house looks forward to my return! the thought popped into Eva's mind as she ruffled Shadow's head and ears. Then she made herself a Turkish coffee with cardamom, one of her favorites, and took it with her to the sofa. She gazed around at the artwork, the sculptures, the items enhancing the living room, each of them representing a specific point of time in her life.

Shadow curled up next to her on the sofa. Yes, she was one of those people who did allow little kids and dogs access to all the furniture in the home. Her husband had sometimes screwed his nose up at it, but she'd always countered with "things are meant to be used, not just displayed." And this led to memories about how her home had bustled with life: four children, their friends, and now their spouses, and some grandkids. A round-the-clock home. No matter what they were doing or where they were, her children knew they could always contact her, even at two in the morning if necessary.

Looking around, she viewed every item with the first lesson's title in mind: everything I see has no meaning. Avraham requested that they spend no more than one minute, twice a day, on each lesson. She looked at the objects in the room once again, trying to grasp the concept of no meaning: the sofa; the large, sculpted lion she had flown in from Thailand and which she thought of as the home's guardian; paintings hung on the wall, some purchased directly from the artists and others that she herself painted when she was younger. She studied each item, which she'd positioned at the time with such love.

How do you relate to a table that isn't a table? A chair that isn't a chair? The array of items which bear names applied by humans, yet what is apparent?

That made her think of a story she'd heard about South American natives. When the ships of Spanish conquistadors reached their shores, the natives didn't oppose them because they'd never seen ships before. They interpreted the vessels as gods of the sea, since that was a familiar phrase passed down through the generations and the only one their minds could apply to what they were witnessing.

Perhaps that which isn't familiar to us and for which we have no name, we haven't read about or learned of, lacks realness? That led Eva to think about the realness of space and what a space contains.

A thought rose in her mind. Space is also what is left when a someone's life has been cut short, for example, in war. She knew of a space like that: her ties to friends from her military service days, earlier adolescence and childhood had all been severed and, it was only when her life shattered that the significance of not having close friends became tangible. She began reconnecting with old acquaintances and, as a result, she learned that the son of a former best friend had been killed in war. Eva found it hard to handle the idea that she hadn't been there for her friend, hadn't offered support, hadn't helped, hadn't grieved with her, given her a shoulder to cry on. She was deeply upset by the idea that someone she'd known from the day he was born, was now 'space.'

But just what is a space? Thinking about her friend's son,

no longer among the living, made Eva wonder about the empty space left in our hearts after the death of someone close to us. Does the space refill? How does one carry on with a chasm in the heart? A difficult concept to perceive because it has no graspable realness. Memories and photos are inadequate substitutes. Since everyone's memories or impressions of a certain person or event are different, perhaps our lives are holograms which lack realness and do not truly hold the significance we apply to them.

Eva remembered a call she'd received on the night-time hotline at the center for sexually abused women. The caller said that, following the abuse she'd experienced, she felt hollow both in body and soul. She felt defiled, physically and mentally, ever since. Inside her being, she bore an empty space, a void, an abyss.

Eva wondered whether the word 'defiled' as used by this woman in the context of sexual abuse would carry the same meaning vis-à-vis religion. If a person felt that their religion had been defiled, was that person not experiencing a personal attack on her or his beliefs, identity, essence? People have always defended their religion, and been killed for doing so. Suddenly the concept of realness, space, non-realness, and how they interlink, was like a bolt of lightning. Perhaps this example would facilitate how to think about the realness or non-realness of objects? And what financial and cultural realness does a person's appearance carry? What about parts of the body? After all, we all inhabit one body in this lifetime. What meaning and interpretation, then, do we apply to our physical appearance?

The words 'hollow gaze' surfaced in Eva's thoughts as she thought of Emily. Was it her sorrowful gaze that attracted Eva to the her? She recalled a staff meeting that occurred about a year after her rude awakening. When the meeting ended, the building contractor, with whom she'd previously worked on a large number of projects, asked her to stay back for a moment.

"I want to talk to you about something," he said. It sounded as though it would be personal. But what could possibly prompt a personal conversation? The contractor walked over to the door, shut it, and sat down facing her.

"For a year now your eyes haven't smiled," he said gently. "You look very troubled, not to mention the weight you've lost. What's going on, Eva? We've known each other for years. Please, feel free to tell me. I hope it's nothing to do with your health."

Startled, Eva's eyes became as big as saucers before she burst into tears. It was the first time she was aware of that someone else noticed the effect of the changes in her life. So she opened up and confided in him. He knew Eva's husband and was taken aback. She never forgot what he said next: "Anything you need, we're here for you. If you need money, if you're having a difficult day coping with clients, we'll cover for you. Whatever we can do to ease things for you a bit, you just let us know. The main thing is that your eyes start smiling again."

Now Eva thought about spaces in her work. Sometimes when she arrived at a location for the purpose of planning a building, she was treading virgin ground. Sometimes trees grew there. Sometimes there was a natural rockery. Sometimes the landscape was urban, sometimes rural. She always noticed scents and whether the land was flat or sloping. That was the external space. By contrast, sometimes she'd arrive at an existing building for which she needed to plan a specific section, small or large. In one way or another, she was causing a deficiency of space.

Humans, Eva thought, shape and form based on what we've learned, what our culture has taught us, and recast space for our own use by absenting it from its original framework. Ancient humans appropriated caves; they didn't carve out space from the external framework but used extant spaces. Only after discovering fire, creating symbols to represent language, and daring to distance them from their nuclear tribe, did humans begin constructing buildings, starting the behavior of space deficits that we continue to enact to this day.

So what is this entity we call 'home'? What meaning does each culture and society bestow to that framework which protects us from heat and cold, from rain and wind? What is the significance of the home's walls, no matter what they're made of: straw, mud, brick or cement block, if terrible actions are carried out inside those walls because no one else can see or hear them? My home is my castle, they say, because that's where we should feel most comfortable, but the walls of this home can also close in on us and imprison our souls.

What then is a bed, with its softness, its comfort, but which can also be a locale of evil? If we come to a momentary understanding that a bed isn't a bed, can we rebuild our approach to the nomenclature of 'bed' despite being victimized on it?

And what about the wall that separates a company's employees' according to hierarchies, such as in offices that Eva plans?

From her work, Eva knows that the height of a divider wall, its degree of opaqueness, whether it has a door for privacy or a window overlooking the outside, form status in others' perceptions, and not just in the perception of the person using that space. Status derives from the culture in which we live, a culture which worships appearances. Eva remembered several instances where employees in a company actually measured the dimensions of a space to ensure that none of them, heaven forbid, would have more than the others, even if the differences were no more than a few centimeters. Do those centimeters define the person? Truly? Does a Rolex watch, the expensive car we drive or the prestigious neighborhood we live in define us, not only outwardly, but inwardly?

From her perspective, the space in which Eva dwelt was full of goodness: the candy of life. And, in a flash, she realized how empty she was inside and how, in a single moment, everything shattered into shards which she was still sweeping.

Right after the 'big bang,' as she thought of it, she badly wanted a close friend to share what she was going through. But, as mentioned, only her children and sister knew of the split between her and her husband. She told no one, not even her parents, about the details of events. To the outside world it seemed nothing had changed. To keep the couple's strife and her internal struggle concealed while keep up the pretense that her family was intact, her husband continued to come for Friday evening dinners. Sometimes she couldn't fathom how it wasn't evident to everyone. Only later she realized that everyone actually had seen, but chose to remain silent.

After divulging to her neighbor what had transpired she felt such relief to know that, beyond her own four walls, someone else would keep an eye out for her. Dita, her neighbor of thirty years, said that she'd heard everything: the crying, the shouting; the absent second car; she'd been waiting for Eva to open the gate between their two gardens and say, "I need help."

Questions raced in Eva's mind, too many for her to grasp.

Exhausted, Eva eventually went to bed, thinking about the lessons she still had to complete by next week's meeting. She pondered her life story: where does it actually begin?

She woke to a new morning. For the first time since her life fell to pieces, she had fallen asleep quickly and didn't wake from nightmares. It was also the first time she hadn't sipped any of the cherry liqueur Dita had given her, so unused to alcohol that the liqueur functioned as an elixir of sleep.

She stared at the picture on the wall hanging in the bedroom, a large poster by the neoclassic artist Ingres of his 1814 painting Grande Odalisque. It depicted a woman reclining, her back to the viewer but her head turned frontward. Eva had purchased it at the Louvre on a trip there some years earlier with her daughter. She and Lily went abroad together at least once a year.

Eva gazed at the image from the perspective of the course.

She sat facing the stunning image thinking about the meaning she applied to it, hanging all these years in her bedroom. Had anyone else in the world with the same image related to it in exactly the same way she did? Does the object have a function? Does memory have meaning? If not for the painting's image visually present, would the memory of that wonderful vacation with her daughter fade?

She wondered if she would ever relocate to a different room, a different place, to a different time. Would this poster go with her?

She let this idea roll about in her mind. Lately she'd started feeling that the house was way too big for her. After all, other than on weekends when her children and parents came to visit, it stood empty, chock full of memories that made it more difficult for her to be there.

Shadow barked loudly. Eva ran to the window to see what was happening outside. She flicked on the outdoor lamps. It was a cloudy spring morning. A darkish morning. Maybe her grandfather's spirit senses something I can't, Eva thought, although it usually communicated with her at night.

Eva was slowly making her way down to her office in the basement when the phone rang. Her ringtone was an excerpt from Baloo's song in the Disney version of Jungle Book: 'The bare necessities of life will come to you.' It was her reminder to head out for a meeting with new clients planning a very large office. Since she was self-employed, had no subordinates, and was only occasionally assisted by external services, she couldn't allow herself to be late, absent or postpone an appointment, no matter how upset she felt.

So there she was, meeting clients as she always did, but her way of looking at space had changed. Every word spoken was imbued with new meaning. She couldn't help thinking that she'd practiced no more than three lessons and it was already leading to a change in her way of thinking. She wondered if the other group members were experiencing something similar. How unusual that she was driven to share her experiences, and with virtual strangers of all people.

And then, suddenly, she wondered why she was hiding her life from others: who was she covering up for? The realization that she'd done nothing wrong slowly began to dawn on her. In fact, why should she care what others say? Her confidence was returning, wrapping itself around her like a warm embrace.

CHAPTER 3

"My mind is preoccupied with past thoughts."

Two weeks had passed since the course's first meeting. For the second meeting Eva decided to arrive some fifteen minutes ahead of time, excited by the first three lessons. She was looking forward to hearing how the others felt when looking around their homes. She wanted to tell Avraham and the group about her thoughts on space and the philosophical concepts that accompanied her during these two weeks. In a great mood, she climbed the stairs to the second floor and made her way to the room where the next session was scheduled.

Stepping inside, she heard voices from the kitchenette adjacent to the classroom. People called her name, invited her in, and smiled at one another like old buddies. There was no sense of awkwardness. Even the room, which was old, shabby, and far from pleasing to Eva's professional eye, took on a different tone. Had her persistence with the homework exercises made her realize that objects only have as much significance as she lends them? Or perhaps it was just the happiness of seeing everyone together again.

Within minutes they'd all crammed into the small kitchen. A sliced cheesecake stood on the counter. It's aroma reminded her of the cheesecakes her mother made. Someone had put herbal tea bags in a bowl. Eva brought mint from her garden. Despite just meeting each other, Eva felt that the group members were connecting easily.

Avraham stepped into the kitchen, took a bit of the cake, and announced that the lesson was about to begin. They all strolled into the classroom, where Avraham signaled for them to sit in a circle.

This time they began with meditation. As always, he gazed intently into the eyes of each of them one by one. Then he asked them to close their eyes, sit up straight, feet firmly on the floor, and he guided them through a five-minute meditation session to relax the body, sending each of them a globe of white light to hold on to for the rest of the session.

"So, how'd the past two weeks go? With what kind of bodily sensations have you arrived to class today, and what senses of physical and emotional energy have you experienced since last we met?"

Answers ranged from confusion to difficulty, excitement to a sense of journey, sleeplessness to pondering, headaches to relief, fear of breaking conventions to fear of the unknown.

"Fear of the unknown is perfectly understandable," Avraham said. "The extant and the past are familiar to us, even if they aren't serving us well now. The moment after we realize that we need to wait for something new, other, is the most threatening moment of all."

That made Eva think of the 'Desert Queen' journey she'd joined, an amazing all-women convoy of ten off-road vehicles traversing Spain's Pyrenees. Firm friendships of the kind that only women can form with each other at the snap of a finger quickly formed there. She remembered how she'd loved taking on the driving challenge over the mountain ridge which was ablaze with the blossoming carpet of June. That morning there'd been a light breeze. June warmth touched the mountain.

Waiting for them was a tremendously long zip-line hung between the sides of two mountains, spanning a vast valley. Below, a river flowed calmly.

Despite her fear, she'd decided, there and then, to take the zip-line challenge. As Avraham had just said, the moment right after the decision is made is the scariest: the second she lifted her legs off the ground. And, instantaneously thereafter, the stunning thrill of freedom.

"As classes progress we'll understand that there's no need to be fearful, because the Shekhinah," he said, using a Hebrew word for God and His presence, "loves us and is always benevolent. Even when we're going through tough stuff, suffering, we'll learn how to find relief, how to view our life narrative from an alternative perspective, and forgive. Forgiveness is the essence of release. When we don't learn to forgive ourselves and others, and see things from another frame of mind, fear of the unknown will continue to seep into us and cannot be overcome."

Eva could feel herself strongly resisting this approach. How does one forgive? How does one forget? How can one ignore things? Avraham's statement had such an impact on her that she felt her body tense.

"Yes, Eva, we will learn how to accomplish this, but not in any way you could possibly imagine right now." Avraham had caught her reaction.

Continuing the discussion, each group member presented the areas that tripped them up or caused them anguish. Sometimes it was a word, sometimes an entire sentence, sometimes an entire chapter roused their distress.

Although no one yet shared their life story, offering no more than a one- or two-sentence glimpse, Eva could feel that this group would indeed be a safe space to expose her emotions without facing judgment.

Nathan asked to talk about a sentence he found disturbing. "I'd like to relate to the sentence 'My mind is preoccupied by past thoughts.' For me it links to what you said earlier, Avraham, about the unknown, about forgiving ourselves and others, and the moment of release. Over the past few years I underwent an emotional process which led me to divorce, and I'll probably go into that more when the right time comes but, for now, I want to only say that I can't lose weight. I know that what is preventing me from dropping those last kilos, getting rid of the medicines and being healthy is the fact that I can't rid the thoughts and questions from the past: What happened? Why? Why did it take so long to leave the house? Why did I accept so many years of suffering?"

"Who doesn't have such thoughts at least once a day?" Avraham asked. "It's a very natural thought pattern because we're human and yet, when this set of thoughts comes up, it's hard to contain, perhaps a little less so at the intellectual level, but very hard at the emotional."

Avraham asked us to go over that lesson once again. "This is an important key to understanding our cognitive and emotional worlds: even though we're the sum of our thoughts, they're only thoughts. When you reread the chapter about how our thoughts attack us, you'll understand how it links to fear of the unknown. As soon as we realize that our thoughts are nothing but just that, thoughts, it gets easier for us to take the next step, even if we don't know where it will lead.

"When you realize," he smiled, "that we're children of the Shekhinah, and that the Shekhinah wants only good for us from the moment we entered the world, the onslaught of thoughts and your fear of the unknown simply dissipate. I know that sounds impossible right now, but remember that we're only at the beginning. Discussing these statements and the changed perspectives in how you relate to the world around you will become a blessing. I know you don't feel that yet. You've got a long way to go, but the moment you feel embraced will be the moment you'll feel tremendous relief."

It was clear from the faces on the group members and how they glanced at each other that they were pretty skeptical. Eva noticed that most were smiling awkwardly. She wondered if they, like she, wondered whether that would really happen.

The concept that anger, frustration, and disappointment in herself for not having seen or properly accessed what was going on could be replaced by understanding, and possibly acceptance, of the fact that ignoring the signs served a purpose at the time seemed simultaneously illogical and, yet, encouraging.

"We tend to think of a specific reality," Avraham explained, "and become angry over it, but maybe getting angry or feeling hurt by it can be viewed differently. All thinking is a type of illusion. So what are we really angry about? Not the action itself, but our thoughts which arise because of the action."

That was definitely an 'aha' moment for many in the group. The class was proving to be another important layer on a ladder that, stage by stage, we would climb even if we dropped back here and there and needed to reclimb some of the rungs. Much later, Eva's inspiration for naming the women's groups she organized 'Ascending the Stairs" came from this class.

"I started understanding my life journey," Eva shared, "over the past two years, as a result of therapy and hearing certain statements repeatedly by my amazing therapist, or from supportive friends or even my sister and wonderful children. 'Look around you,' they'd say, 'and see the good in your surroundings. Look at what you've given to the world.' Maybe when we allow ourselves to hover above the difficulty, we can slowly realize that we hold the choice of how to view everything.

"I think that's as true," Eva continued, "for our private lives as it is for how we integrate into society, into a nation, into a country. I'm only now beginning to comprehend that what happened doesn't define me, that emotions that attack me do so because I enabled them to do so." That brought to mind the lesson she'd read some days earlier, titled 'My attack thoughts are affecting my invulnerability.'

"After what you said, Avraham, about forgiveness and experiencing a moment of release once we understand our life trajectory via an alternative perspective, by thinking differently, or perhaps with added layers of our understanding of life, I texted my therapist and told her how hard it was for me to accept that. I saw myself as a strong, successful, attractive woman, who's loved; a mother, a grandmother, who gives her all, is creative, cares for others; a loving and beloved daughter; and yet I'm the one who let myself be attacked? Why is it that I let myself only view my life from a single perspective?

"My therapist answered that she really gets what I'm saying, that it's the hardest idea to handle. But she also wrote how certain she is that group work will enable me to get a better grasp on things and attain even the emotional relief that I so deeply want."

"Right. So let's practice understanding how vulnerability and invulnerability are outcomes of our thoughts," Avraham prompted and turned to face Emily, who was gazing off into space and had hardly said a word. "Emily, give it a shot and try to say an attack statement to Sarai."

Sarai, who had also sat withdrawn since the session's start, jerked her head up, clearly feeling awkward.

Emily was taken aback by being pressed to think of a way to attack Sarai. They were both so introverted that we knew hardly anything about them. Sarai had told us a few snippets in the kitchen earlier on: that she married very young, has four successful adult children, and when the last left she'd experienced the crisis in her couplehood, since her husband had retired and she wasn't employed either.

Emily, by contrast, was a long-time divorcee. Her kitchen chatter the previous week had informed us that she had three children, that she was pleased with them, but that she was hiding a story that she couldn't yet share.

Avraham asked her to think of a situation in her life when she was furious, and try to talk from that stance. She really had difficulty. She could hardly get her voice out. Tears began flowing. Sarai, sitting opposite her, cringed more and more. We watched these two adult women, mothers, unable to look each other in the eye, certainly not to lash out with an attack statement, even if only for the sake of the exercise.

"You hurt me. You stopped me from living my life to the full," Emily finally blurted through her tears. Sarai was visibly moved, as though the words pierced her soul. Emily breathed deeply, horrified at the fact that she'd actually gone ahead and said something that had been weighing heavily on her heart.

"Do we let others hurt us?" I persisted, directing the question to Avraham. "What if a child is raped? Or a woman is physically or emotionally abused?"

"We'll need to progress in the book to understand that even if horrific events are enacted," Avraham said, "like those Eva's described, or terrible events of wars, harsh diseases or loss of a child in an accident, the way we rehabilitate our lives and live that truth is dependent on our decision. Each person has their own way: either sinking and disappearing, immersing in the harsh memory, fuming, foregoing life, or deciding that life's worth living and that, since the sun and moon will shine and the stars will sparkle even if our physical or emotional world has fractured, we can find a way to live alongside the fracture."

On our coffee break we chatted about how some people who underwent true horrors managed to rebuild their lives and live them to their fullest, whereas others collapse, become addicted to alcohol or drugs, and keep on hurting their families despite countless promises to stop, and how this can turn into a never-ending loop of intergenerational transference.

Some of us, as the children of Holocaust survivors, understood that idea so well.

The evening ended with discomfort. Surfacing questions were bothersome.

"This hasn't been a simple lesson but, if you practice it at home over the coming week and keep moving ahead with the next classes, you'll soon take it in stride," Avraham said.

CHAPTER 4

"Above all else I want to see."

Eva arrived for the next class. Despite having practiced the material, she was still having plenty of difficulty. From the kitchen chats she learned that most of the group members were in the same boat.

"If any of you want to make a statement or share, please feel free," Avraham opened the class. "It may not be easy, but try to listen without offering advice or interjecting remarks. Just listen. It's an opportunity to practice being in this state and learning the difference between hearing and listening. Try to focus on that difference."

David decided to speak up.

"I grew up in an ultra-Orthodox neighborhood, one of the most extreme, called Neturei Karta. For those who don't know, it actually means 'guardians of the city' referring, of course, to Jerusalem's spiritual aspects. The neighborhood is like an old-style ghetto, houses packed one top of the other without a sliver of privacy, zealously maintained uniformity of dress, no room for self-expression, everything's dictated from the moment you wake at sunrise to the moment you go to sleep. The only place I could let my thoughts fly was in my dreams," he grimaced, "because no one's figured out how to control our minds."

"Already as a little kid it bothered me that my parents were so opposed to the country they were living in, yet freely used its buses and taxis, bought in its shops, received child endowment and other social services, and funds from the very Zionist entity they professed to loathe. I love my family. I love the books of the Torah and exegeses, I always excelled at the *kheider* and Talmud Torah."

He paused, realizing that not everyone was familiar with those words. "These ultra-Orthodox groups only study Jewish texts. So, kheider is like elementary school but for Jewish texts only, no secular materials such as math, science, and English at all—it's all learned through Torah texts. And Talmud Torah equates, I guess, with high school but, again, no secular subjects, only highly advanced Torah studies."

He leaned back in his chair. "But the doubts never left me." He told the group that one day he decided on a secret trip 'beyond the ghetto boundaries' to a library he'd heard about, the main library of a community center, where one of the librarians took him under her wing. She gave him books about philosophy and sciences, about far-flung cultures and different religions.

"That librarian and I... we had so many conversations. I was comfortable talking to her because she herself had grown up as part of a different ultra-Orthodox sect. Her father was an Orthodox Rabbi who led a community. She understood the prohibition against males and females who are not married to each other being alone in a closed space and always made sure that the library door, or her office door, was open. We could talk in undertones but we never breached that prohibition.

"I told her about my siblings and my older sister, who showed unusual curiosity about things not from our world, but I never had the guts to talk openly with her about my ideas. She's only a year older and is a fabulous artist and illustrator. One day I noticed that she wasn't only drawing permissible images such as saintly Rabbis and ritual artefacts. I realized that I'd seen forbidden images and it scared me like crazy. Maybe I was more surprised at discovering that this non-permissible line of thinking ran in the family and I wasn't the only one dealing with it."

"The librarian smiled and said she understood completely. She told me that, as a teen, she fell in love with a guy who wasn't part of her parents' sect and they refused point blank to let her marry him. She never married after that because she couldn't get that young fellow out of her heart even though they'd hardly exchanged a word, maybe a few sentences here and there, some surreptitious glances at each other in the supermarket or through the screen separating men from women in the synagogue.

"She said that he eventually married a girl from his own sect. Sometimes she'd lie in bed wondering if he thought about her. Although she'd see him on the street on occasion, she never looked straight at him. 'I think that these days my parents would behave differently,' she told me."

He stopped for a few sips of water before continuing. "On one hand, the librarian encouraged me to go with my heart, especially after telling me about her life. On the other hand, I didn't have the gumption to stand up to my community. I knew it would break my parents, and also cause tons of trouble in the future, especially for my younger sisters. But eventually I broke and decided to leave it all. It was as though the devil himself had slipped into my body.

"At some point I stopped going to the library. Later I learned that the librarian tried using her contacts in our neighborhood to find out what happened to me and even attempted to 'smuggle' a book to me, but I didn't respond. In retrospect, I learned that I wasn't the only one spending time at the library. I married in a pre-arranged betrothal, as is usual for our sect, but I really love and admire my wife Ruth, the mother of my kids. And I completed my Jewish studies at the Kollel, the tertiary level seminary for married men."

Listening to him was so strange. He spoke in everyday language with a bit of current slang thrown in that was nothing like the way members of his sect would speak. In one of the pre-class kitchen gatherings he said he was in hi-tech and lived in the bustling center of Tel Aviv. Eva's family counted some ultra-Orthodox folk among them, and she picked up on the typical way the men often swayed lightly when concentrating, a habit common when praying or studying. It was most evident in David when he was emotional. Markers of his religious lifestyle were visible: his skullcap and the ritual fringes hanging out from under his shirt. His jeans were definitely not in line with the ultra-Orthodox attire, but typical of hi-techers of course. It was clear we were all fascinated, never having expected such a story, and we waited keenly for him to carry on.

"After our first child was born, I couldn't live this lie anymore, certainly not with my wife and any future children we'd have. So I shared my concerns with Ruth. I was stunned. She said she felt the same way! It turns out that she'd also never told anyone what was deep in her heart, never expressed her true thoughts or the fact that she'd walk around parts of the city considered out of bounds, pop into shops, amazed by how colorful everything was, by the abundance, by the huge array of choices of clothing and items. She said she had a long talk with a warmhearted woman who noticed Ruth standing outside her boutique's display window. The woman noticed how distressed Ruth appeared and invited her in.

"Some of the boutique clients were surprised to see Ruth there. She was covered head to toe in black and her tight black cap left not even a single wisp of hair visible. Some of the women also joined the conversation about what is permitted and prohibited, about what's good in a life where everything is predetermined but also how it doesn't necessarily suit all personalities, how the imprisonment of thoughts is no longer befitting to the world we now live in, and how Ruth's dream of becoming a lawyer was unacceptable in her ultra-Orthodox community. Ruth had always felt that law was where she could give free rein to her linguistic and logical capabilities, as well as her wish to promote justice and equality for ultra-Orthodox women in society.

"But any time she muttered a word about it to her parents, they'd simply locked her up for days at a time, literally imprisoned in her own home, until she realized she'd have to archive the dream. She promised her parents that she'd marry a man of their choosing and would get 'all that silly nonsense about social equality' out of her head."

Although David's voice remained calm, he was clearly very moved by what he was telling us. "The moment I told Ruth how torn I was as well, she said that perhaps her prayers went to the right ears and brought her the man who'd free her mind from captivity."

A smile spread across David's face and his voice took on a fuller, more gratified tone. "For me that was a moment of pure joy. I was beside myself. I felt uplifted in a way that no studies or prayers ever stirred. I told her about Yvette, the librarian, and suggested we both go to talk to her and seek her advice. I also thought about exposing Ruth to the 'forbidden' books."

Well, isn't that interesting! Eva noted. My cousin Yvette is a librarian and from an ultra-Orthodox home. Could it be possible...? But Eva didn't give it any more thought and focused on David, who was continuing his story.

"Yvette decided to help us. She saw it as a kind of mission. Ever since her own life was impacted by the community's rigidity, she decided to help anyone in similar circumstances who approached her looking for a way out of their angst. She was connected with 'Hillel,' an organization that helped people like us gently integrate into the world beyond our boundaries, understanding the price we'd pay for our choice, such as the loss of contact with the family, the price our siblings would pay when it came to finding them matches, and so on. But her support and that of many other kind people helped us leave our street, our ghetto, and move to a more open and religious, but not ultra-religious, neighborhood.

"Both families experienced a greater crisis than we could have imagined. Both sat the seven day mourning period for us as though we were dead. Ruth and I were beside ourselves with sorrow. In one fell swoop we were disconnected from everything we'd known: friends, siblings, extended family. We were labeled 'untouchables.' That's when I told Ruth about my sister Rosie. That I noticed when she was young that she also had a tendency towards 'the forbidden' and what a shame I never had the guts to tell her where my thoughts lie.

"Now it's too late. My parents must have guessed where things were heading and sent her to Brooklyn, New York, where they arranged a match. She has eight kids and is deeply entrenched in the countless details of keeping a large family running. From my correspondence with her, I can tell that she's unhappy, but I never had the courage to ask her how she felt.

"Meanwhile Ruth and I have two more little ones. We gave them more modern Jewish names, unlike the biblical name we gave Rebecca, our firstborn. The boys are six and seven years old. We're doing well in our new neighborhood, I completed all my secular studies and started working in hi-tech. Ruth caught up on her secular studies and has a Bachelor of Law. So she did realize her big dream. She specializes in intellectual property law. She felt that this field would allow her to help others stand up for their rights which manifest in creative activities such as music, literature, art, photography, patents, and so on. Maybe it drew her because our own life experiences, linked to the limitations enforced on our intellects as youngsters.

"There's harmony in our little family. But there's also a ton of hardship," David sighed. "The coerced distancing from our nuclear families is unbearable. Ruth started adopting some ultra-Orthodox behaviors in the hope that this would restore the relationship with our parents. I agreed and even cooperated with her. For me it was like dressing up, putting on a costume, but I knew how important it was to Ruth. Now, we're on the spectrum of religious, tending toward ultra-Orthodox, but nonetheless live in an area that is accepting of a whole array of religious observance.

"Our families did restore ties with us. Life has been moving along pleasantly this past year, but I agonize inside. It makes me feel that I'm once again lying to my soul and my family. A therapist I secretly visited helped me with the decision to join this course. I found that the book allows for my soul's deliberations and was happy to meet you all. I registered without telling Ruth and, the truth is, I don't even know why I hid it. Maybe I was worried about crossing the boundaries for the second time in my life and involved in a secret activity that excites me.

"So I read ahead and reached lesson 27, which talks about wanting to see more than anything else. And that spoke to me. As the first sentence of that lesson explains, it's more forceful than decisiveness. It prioritizes my vision over my wishes, and that scares me to death. I had trouble simply saying the words, 'vision has no cost to anyone' because I feel like my heart is paying a humongous price. I'm lying to my wife, who walked the walk with me step by step, but didn't go as far as I did. She's got her feet firmly planted on the ground, she's more practical but, the fact is, she chose to resume some of the more orthodox practices. She couldn't completely turn her back on them."

David halted, looked up at the ceiling momentarily, and sighed. "Me, I want full release. I want to live a fully secular life. I'm more of a dreamer, less down to earth and pragmatic, even though I'm a programmer. I look for meaning in everything. Ruth is more rigid, accepts things as they are. I believe that her childhood, with its rigid framework, has nonetheless influenced her because, despite it all, she found it hard to let go.

"A couple of days ago Ruth found the book. I don't know how I wasn't more careful. Probably, subconsciously, I wanted her to find 'A Course in Miracles.' Deep inside I felt sure Ruth would have difficulty with the book, but I felt like a rebel, like the kid who went off secretly to the library, like a confused and scared little boy. Only problem is: I'm not a kid," he smiled and a tear slid down his cheek. "I'm an adult, a man married to a woman I love, and father to children who are my whole world."

How different is that, Eva thought, from a man who cheats on his wife and leaves signs and markers around but his wife doesn't see them? Or maybe she chooses not to see them. She could feel tears falling from her own eyes.

"So Ruth told me that she began reading the book. She wondered if she could connect to it and be a partner in it and understand what I was going through, but she was horrified when she realized the book came via Jesus. That was too much for her. She thinks I've gone too far and is insisting I stop joining the classes—otherwise she'll demand a divorce."

David clasped and unclasped his hands, shifted in his seat, and picked the book up from his lap. He clutched the book as though gripped by disappointment at not finding an answer to what he was going through. It was hard to watch him. Eva had an urge to sit next to him and tell him how much she empathizes with this sensitive pivot, where he found a way to live his life yet something external was preventing him from fulfilling it.

"For the sake of family harmony, for the sake of my wife whom I love, for my children's sake, I've decided to leave the course." Tears flowed down his cheeks as he spoke. "I could see Ruth was deeply hurt, not so much by me registering for the course as the fact that I hid it from her. We'd already begun taking such significant steps in our lives, turning to each other over anything that bothered us, and here I am back in that childhood status of doing things on my own and not sharing them with her. That's what broke her."

We were all shaken by his revelation. No one had imagined that this is how David's story would conclude. For some reason we'd all expected it to end by him saying that Ruth eventually came around to the idea that she might even join the next class. But that's for movies, not for real life. The group members sat quietly, upset at not being able to help, especially since Avraham had requested that we listen without any kind of response. Not responding was tough.

"Let's take a coffee break and recharge our energy," Avraham suggested.

That was Eva's chance to approach David.

"Can we go outside for a second?" she smiled at him. "I'd like to ask you a question but Sharon's bracelets clinking constantly distract me." Sharon's typical lateness when joining or rejoining the group, and the accompanying clinking, unsettled Eva, breaking her concentration. Eva had a sense it affected the others, too. "I sometimes really want to ask Avraham to request that she doesn't come with them to the meetings," she added. David nodded in agreement.

"Even though I grew up in a secular home," Eva began, "most of my extended family are Orthodox or ultra-Orthodox. Most are highly educated and openminded and the family, as a whole, is very united. Do you remember the librarian's family name?"

"Of course. Yvette Ehrlich," David answered without hesitation.

Eva's cousin!

"Why not call her, even though years have passed, and try to set up a meeting with her and Ruth?" Eva suggested, watching David's face. "She went back to a religious lifestyle. Did you know that? You probably remember her also as very open-minded, and maybe now that she's resumed religious practices, she can help Ruth understand that even though the book came through spiritual communication with Jesus, it has so much to offer. In all honesty, it troubled me quite a bit at first, too," Eva admitted, "but I simply decided that every time I see the word 'Jesus' in the book, I'd swap it in my mind for 'Shekhinah' and that works brilliantly."

"Thanks. I appreciate it," David answered. "Maybe one day I'll muster up enough courage to ask Ruth if she'll come with me for a conversation with Yvette. But right now things are very shaky between us and I first need to rehabilitate our relationship and regain her trust. Maybe talking to Yvette could be the next step." When the meeting ended, David made his farewells. We wished him success in bridging the rift with his wife and finding an alternative outlet for what was bothering him. Eva found it hard to see David's distress. She could sense what he was feeling: a person who didn't love himself, who isn't happy, who repeatedly senses that every step forward actually brings him back to behaviors he knew as a child, and trying to gratify others.

"I hope that one day you'll find wholeness in yourself," Eva wished him, "and be able to live with Ruth and raise your children to make choices that will enrich them. If not, we diminish our own basic right to happiness while simultaneously preventing ourselves from granting it to others."

On the drive home Eva turned her comments to David round and round in her thoughts. His story weighed heavily on her. She thought about the family relationship, the fact that he wasn't willing to forego it because the family unit was more important to him than anything else. She was envious. For the next three days she walked around the house with a raging headache.

When the Friday evening meal came around, the family chose a restaurant for celebrating one of the son's birthday. Despite the split, they decided that birthdays would still be celebrated together as a family. Tossing the idea around in her mind, Eva concluded that at the end of the restaurant meal, she'd ask her husband to set aside time for a private conversation. She knew she'd be taking a huge risk, realizing that he was probably continuing his liaison with the other woman, but David's words had engraved themselves in her mind.

The family settled themselves around the restaurant table. Eva always knew what would please each of her children though, technically speaking, they lacked for nothing. But she could always find that specific gift they'd love, would make them smile and so, unsurprisingly, she'd found something special for celebrating her son's birthday.

The food was wonderful; everyone complimented the chef. She did her best to barely look at her husband, who was seated opposite her, and focus more on her children. Perhaps she feared what might eventuate. Desert and birthday cake eaten, she presented the gift from both his parents and began to read out the card. She'd always written up celebratory wishes and evening her husband's speeches for his various conferences. "With love, from Mom and Dad," the card ended. And that ended the meal. The family rose to leave.

"One sec," she said quietly to her husband. "I'd like to talk to you." The rest of the family quickly caught on and left. Eva sat down again opposite her husband and took a deep breath. She wanted to reach his heart; perhaps he would reconsider the separation, perhaps they could try again, even though both had experienced two difficult years, perhaps for the sake of the family unit that would be forever disbanded, they could give greater weight to the good things they shared.

A moment before she could said a word, he spoke; his words carried intense anger and Eva was shocked.

"Do you think I don't get what you're doing? Do you really think I'm such a total idiot? You wrote out the congratulatory wishes in first person, from you, yourself, even though the gift was from both of us. Only at the end you added 'Dad.' Do you really think no one noticed that?"

Eva sat in stunned silence. She hadn't expected such a toxic accusation.

"Right. So what did you want to talk to me about?" he asked.

Eva stood abruptly, pushing the chair back so hard that it almost fell. At the last second she remembered her tote hanging on its backrest. She spun around, not wanting him to see the tears welling in her eyes.

"Nothing," she said at almost a whisper, leaving the restaurant and letting the door slam behind her, to a nearby waiter's shock. The children were still hanging around near their cars, chatting with each other, which is how they saw her bawling as she walked to her own car.

"What happened?" one of them ran over, worried.

"Everything's fine," she muttered. "I'll be fine. You can go home."

What an upsetting way for the birthday meal to end. She'd been looking forward to it, and hoped that talking to her husband might induce a change. But in that moment of clarity brought about by his response she realized that, despite her life being packaged as happy, it was empty of self-love. Here she was, again willing to forego herself for her family's sake. Behind the wheel, she sat thinking about how, for years, she'd given up on her friends, on heart-to-heart talks, the kind that allow for discomfort, including the unsettling feelings of the past few years. She'd always thought of such talks as unproductive. Why would she waste time on talking with a friend in a café?

She decided to clear the morning and dedicate it to herself. She would phone the project manager, who knew about her current situation, and ask him to cover for her and conduct the check on the special ceilings for the boardroom. Then she'd phone a childhood friend and see if they could meet up.

She drove through a torrent of tears, a commonplace driving mode over the past couple of years. She decided that, at the next Miracles meeting, she'll talk about her life story. She let herself into the house and headed for her work desk to draft a list of bullet points.

That done, she curled up on the sofa with the book and continued reading. She was strongly drawn to the lessons on seeing the world through her own eyes, particularly the concept of 'I have invented the world I see.'

Eva practiced that lesson throughout the week. "I invented reality the way I see it," she kept repeating to herself.

She could feel her resistance to this statement every time she said it. She had trouble coming to terms with the idea that, even if certain actions weren't entirely under her control or she'd cooperated unconsciously, she was still the one who chose how to see them. She chose the perspective. She found it difficult to comprehend that her husband was giving up on her, giving her up, continuing his life without her. Even if she knew, intrinsically, how to behave under the circumstances, her ego was screeching in opposition.

That morning she was woken by a surprising phone call, someone she hadn't heard from for well over two decades.

"Gaia? Eva asked.

"Eva?" the voice answered. Eva grinned from ear to ear.

"Gaia, your call came at exactly the right time," Eva said with sincerity.

"I ran into Michelle yesterday. Remember her? Anyhow, I just thought I'd give you a buzz and see what's doing."

They decided to meet later that morning.

Sitting in the café, Gaia talked about the ups and downs of her life, which ran along startingly similar lines to Eva's. The conversation flowed as though they'd never stopped being in touch. When they said their goodbyes, Eva's eyes swam with tears. Suddenly she realized what she'd missed all these years: a call from a friend, a chat in a café, the opportunity to talk and be heard, to air views, to get responses. To enjoy being together.

The day before the next meeting, Avraham texted, "Got time to talk?

"Sure," she answered, even though she was taken by surprise. "For you, anytime!"

"I know you were looking forward to telling your story tomorrow," he said when they spoke, "but an hour ago Yoli phoned and said she's in a terribly stressful situation and needs the group's and my help tomorrow. I understand and hear what you're feeling now, but if you can let Yoli take tomorrow's slot, I'd be very grateful."

Listening to Avraham, Eva's stomach churned. First, she could feel herself straining against the idea. That she would feel so much resistance upset her. She didn't know what to say. He heard the hesitant silence.

"Bottom line, it's your decision," he said, "and I know you were looking forward to speaking."

She took a deep breath before talking.

"It's really hard for me," she eventually said, "because, from childhood, I've been related to as a good little girl, a pretty girl, pleasant, calm, I don't push myself in forcefully, I don't stand out, I forego to others whose need is greater, a girl who is present but transparent. And finally, during this recent period and the process I'm going through, I understand that even if, seemingly, I'm transparent, that's not the case at all. It was the story I was telling myself."

She hesitate but came to a quick decision. "But alright. Tell Yoli that she can have tomorrow and I'll take a different day. And..."

The pause lengthened weightily. "And, you know, suddenly I don't feel as though I'm giving up my turn due to being invisible or absent, but out of self-awareness and strength."

Suddenly Eva understood that the statement she'd been repeating about 'inventing the world she sees' was helping her to make important decisions, even if they weren't always the most pleasant ones.

CHAPTER 5

"God is the love in which I forgive."

Right after the prolonged meditation commencing the meeting, Avraham apologized and thanked Eva for having waived her request to share and gave the floor to Yoli.

Yoli began hesitantly, nodding a look of gratitude Eva's way.

"I started reading ahead on the lessons, as Avraham recommended we do if we're looking for answers. I don't know whether my story contains forgiveness of others or, perhaps, thankfulness, and I'm very confused about that.

"I'm adopted. My parents were born in Hungary. My mother comes from Cluj in Transylvania, which is now part of Romania."

That made Eva's ears prick up: Eva's mother was born in that same city.

"My parents met after the Second World War, when each was returning to their hometown. My mother said that she rode the trains with several young women who had stayed together in the concentration camps. My mother and another friend were given 'treatments' by Mengele," Yoli said, referring to the infamous officer and physician known as 'The Angel of Death' at Auschwitz for his horrific experiments on children and youth in general, and their reproductive organs in particular.

"My mother told me that, one day, the Germans simply all disappeared from the concentration camp and she and the other experimental patients found themselves alone, not understanding what was happening. The camp was liberated. She and her friends decided to run away and never believe anyone ever again. They weren't even going to enter the assimilation center which the liberators set up for them. So instead, they boarded a freight train, then switched to another, hiding in the carriages. They would get off some place, take clothing from clothes lines, eat whatever they could find in the fields or along the roadside, and continue their journey back home, avoiding contact with people in general but especially with men.

"On the way, some of the girls left the group and went off in different directions. It took a long time for my mother and her girlfriend to get back to their hometown. She couldn't remember exactly how long the traveling took. Back in their city, they discovered that absolutely nothing remained of the streets where they'd lived. Neither of them had any photos of their families, not a single memento. They heard about a center set up in the city by a group of people from the Land of Israel who were aiding refugees by providing food and lodgings and, eventually, helping them emigrate there. Both wanted that. They'd been raised in open-minded religious homes and had been members of religious Zionist youth groups.

"For the most part, Cluj had been known for tolerance among the different religions; their community's Rabbi had supported the Zionist movement. When they were eventually settled into an absorption center near their hometown, my mother met my father, who also came from Cluj. He was twenty years her elder and had lost his entire family in Auschwitz. They felt an instant click and married fairly quickly. Perhaps their shared fate brought them together. At the time, the age difference wasn't felt at all. What they wanted was connection, love, warmth, someone to care for them. The feelings of loss, emptiness, heartbreak and weary broken bodies were so tough. My mother said that plenty of people got together simply because they wanted to feel human again, to feel part of a larger unit, to love, to have children and, in that way, beat the cursed Nazis."

As Yoli talked, Eva sat, mouth agape with incredulity. This felt like déjà -vu, as though her own mother was telling this very same story.

"A while later they were sent in trains paid for by Jewish organizations that helped anyone in Europe wanting to emigrate to Israel. They reached Split, a seaport in the city of Lid, Yugoslavia, where they waited their turn to board a boat carrying the refugees. In July 1947, they boarded a Haganah ship called 'Exodus.' It eventually docked at Haifa after being halted by the British. But the refugees on board kicked up such a rebellion that the Brits let it through and the refugees were taken to the nearby port of Atlit."

"Once they were released from the temporary refugee camp at Atlit, my mother's friend went to a kibbutz and my parents stayed in Tel Aviv. Even though my father knew my mother couldn't have children after Mengele's so-called experiments, he loved her deeply. So they decided to try adoption. They stayed in contact with my mother's friend but the connection grew weaker over time. A year later, in July, I was born to a young, ultra-Orthodox girl who had stayed in Jerusalem until giving birth in what one would call a home for wayward girls. My biological mother never agreed to provide the father's name. She only said that the young man from her neighborhood studied in a Yeshiva," Yoli said, using the Hebrew for a seminary for men.

"My parents adopted me when I was a week old. They called me Yoli because I was born in July, but explained that it was also the name of someone very close to them who guided and assisted them throughout the adoption process, the waiting time and the adoption itself.

"My parents were loving people and happy, despite the

Holocaust's horrors. They educated me to love my fellow man and did all they could to provide me with everything I could possibly need but, all my life, I felt that there was something more about my mother's barrenness that distressed her, something she'd never shared with me. Despite the pain and longing for her family, all murdered in the Holocaust, she sometimes spoke about her parents as though she bore a grudge. Neither she nor my father ever delved into that, though."

"I served in the military in an important role in the intelligence corps. There, the advantage of my parents talking to me in both German and Hungarian was useful. Did they speak to me in their native tongues because they wanted to preserve an aspect of their childhoods? Or, in some way, pay tribute to the places that ended up being so cruel to them, preventing them from experiencing adolescence? I don't know. But they were extremely proud of me, were always supportive. And the truth is that I was indeed a good daughter.

"Both my parents are light-haired and have blue eyes, whereas I, as you see, have pitch-black hair and dark-brown eyes; but, because from early childhood I knew I was adopted, I never dug into the story. My life was good, and I was loved so much. I never felt like an outsider in the family unit.

"I met my husband when we both studied pharmacology at university. He was in the year above me. We met in the library and from first glance felt tremendously drawn to each other. From my perspective, pharmacology was as close as I could get to medicine, which had been my father's dream. One that growing up in a poverty-struck village, and then the Holocaust, never let him achieve."

"Madly in love, we married and have our own successful pharmacy. We're very open with each other and so happy together. We have three children who loved my parents, and my parents loved them too. The same is true for my husband's family, which connected warmly with my own. My husband's from a large, bustling Moroccan family, which instantly provided me with a big loving clan."

Eva squirmed on her seat yet again. She'd been doing that a lot during Yoli's story. Avraham was probably the only one who'd noticed, but could never imagine how the day would end. Yoli, on the other hand, looking around at everyone, noticed the expressions on their faces: if everything is so good, why are you in the group?

"Some years ago my mother was diagnosed with breast cancer. My father was beside himself. He and I and the entire extended family banded together to help, to be there for her, to give her back a little of what she'd given to us all so warmly and lovingly. My mother's friend, who'd helped her through the harsh Holocaust years, came to visit. She was deeply pained by my mother's illness and helped and supported her a good deal. My mother fought until the disease eventually took her life two years ago. Now I was orphaned of my mother who'd been my whole world.

"My father was heartbroken. From a tall man whose age never showed, whose vitality was evident, he quickly grew old. He'd never thought his wife would die before him. A year ago he fell desperately ill. We rallied to support him. One day he told me that he has to tell me a story, something to do with my mother. He sat down facing me, took my hands in his now bony ones, and said that right before the Germans invaded Hungary, her parents took her to a gynecologist, where they sterilized her. At the time, they had connections with the Jewish hospital, which was also the most advanced in Hungary. Her parents said the procedure was for her own benefit. She didn't have a clue what was actually being done.

"It seems rumors had reached Hungary about how the concentration camps were run: that Jewish women were forced to become sex slaves to the Nazis, especially if they were pretty. And she was: blond, slim, petite, not at all the typically dark-haired, dark-eyed Jewish girl. My mother's parents were convinced that neither of them would survive the war or be able to watch over her, and they wanted to protect her from giving birth to a child resulting from rape. Only when she survived and discovered what her parents had done did she realize that they'd actually sentenced her to a life without children.

"It was so hard for me to absorb. 'You were the light of our life!' my father told me. 'After having lost my wife and children, and your mother losing the privilege of giving birth, you came to us like a little angel, healing our wounds.' My father died a year ago and is buried next to my mother.

"When we were clearing the house, we found a faded photo in the pocket of one my father's trousers: a woman and two children, no doubt his family murdered in the Holocaust. He always said he had no photos... maybe he wanted to keep the memory of his first wife and children to himself. I never opened my adoption file. I never felt driven to do that. But since my father told me about my mother, the story doesn't let me rest. I love my parents dearly, but my insides are a mess, torn between hugging my mother when she was alive and saying thank you for choosing me and understanding that, her entire life, she was angry at her parents and perhaps couldn't help imagining what her biological children might look like had her parents not forced her to be sterilized. Maybe she viewed me as a compromise.

"I can't help thinking over and over that had my grandparents not carried out the sterilization, I wouldn't have been privileged to have those two people as my parents. Then suddenly I went from being a woman certain of my parents' love, to feeling estranged. An image keeps running through my mind: my mother stroking her belly and imagining how her children would look. I try to shoo the image away. I don't know whether to open the adoption file and discover who my biological mother is and then wonder if I have other half siblings, or simply let it be and accept that my parents chose me, they loved me to bits and, even if my mother was badly treated and my father lost his first family, I'm the one who brought them joy, just as my father said before he passed away.

"From living a happy, loving and very gratifying life, I've gone to sleepless nights, unable to figure out what I should be thinking and how to retell myself the story of my birth. At night, in the dark, I repeat this like a mantra: 'God is the love in which I forgive you, Mother' and 'God is the love in which I forgive myself' and 'God is the love in which I am blessed.' I seem to need to forgive my mother, who loved me like crazy, and then I feel terrible for having these angry thoughts towards my parents, for I know that I really am blessed for having had two parents like that."

Heart wrenching sobs burst from Yoli. Eva began to stand, wanting to go and comfort her, but Avraham signaled to sit back down.

"Avraham, it's okay, really," Eva said.

"Alright," he nodded, sensitive to the situation.

Eva sat on the floor, cupping Yoli's knees in her palms.

"I'm sitting here listening to your story," Eva spoke softly to Yoli, "and as you continue, I realize that I know your story from up close, from my home. Your name is Yoli, with an 'o' and not a 'u'; the same name as my mother's Hungarian name. She is your mother's friend, the same one who went through the Holocaust together with your mother. My mother is still alive and would certainly be happy to talk to you. She never told me or my sister or any of the grandchildren what they went through there. She's not well, but she's at home and I'm sure she'd love to see you. Perhaps a hug from her, or a talk, will ease your soul. All of us here together can help each other find that relief and forgiveness we all need in our lives." With that, Eva burst into tears.

The group was in a state of shocked silence. Initially Yoli

couldn't make sense of what Eva had said, but suddenly her eyes opened wide and she burst into tears. Eva and Yoli hugged like two lost sisters to mothers who shared their lives and secrets.

Avraham decided to end the meeting at this point, and asked the group members to keep reading ahead and sharing difficulties they encountered on the group WhatsApp.

Eva was actually pleased that there'd be no classes for the coming two weeks. "Would you like to meet my mother and father?" she asked Yoli.

"Yes, I'd be very happy to," Yoli answered.

"Let me talk to my father first and see if he thinks my mother can cope with the meeting, okay?"

"Of course."

Interestingly, when she phoned her father he suggested she check directly with her mother but that, if she agreed, not to pressure her with all kinds of questions. Rather, let the meeting develop at its own pace.

Eva went to her parents' home. She sat next to her mother, whose Hebrew name was Hannah but whom everyone called Nana. Eva noticed how much her mother's hands trembled. More than usual.

"Mom," she said, holding her hand gently, "remember I told you that I'm doing a course that could bring miracles to our lives?"

Her mother nodded. "Yes, and I still say that I don't understand why you need such a course. Your life is perfect. You've even lost some weight lately."

"That's due to my husband," Eva said cynically, her mother's raised eyebrow showing she didn't understand Eva's jibe. "Anyhow, I wanted to tell you about something amazing that happened to me with one of the women in yesterday's session. I think you know her well."

My mother gave me a questioning glance but her hand and mind relaxed. Eva continued. "I met Yoli, the daughter of your friend Evie, there." The look on her mother's face was unreadable. Eva looked around at her father, who nodded, signaling her to continue. "Yoli would be thrilled to meet you, Mom. We both understand that there's a whole lot more to the story, concealed within your long history together from childhood until your immigration to Israel and afterwards. Do you think you could talk to Yoli and me at least about some of the story?"

"Ah, yes I'd be happy to!" Eva's mother agreed. "I saw Yoli for just a few moments shortly before Evie passed away," she added before falling silent. She hadn't been able to attend the mourning period at their home. It would have been too painful.

Eva's mother had never shared the details of what she'd been through in the Holocaust. She had spoken of the moment she was separated from her mother and sisters once they reached the train platform at Auschwitz; how she tried to take an infant from another woman so that she'd look older and let her go with her mother, but Mengele noticed, slapped her hard, and moved her to the other line of people, the ones who would live. She said that, in the blink of an eye, she saw her father Yekutiel and her three brothers: Benzi, Yehuda and Moshe; and then her mother Naomi, in her red dress with white polka dots, her younger sister, Haya, and her baby sister, Nushi. And that was the last time she saw any of them.

After that, the only thing she remembered was the stench from the crematorium burning the Jews.

It was the last year of the war. Everyone knew as they disembarked from the train what awaited them when the Germans screeched at them and the dogs barked furiously. But she never shared more, she never described what happened up to the moment she boarded 'Exodus.' For Eva, it was all a great black hole.

A lightbulb went on in Eva's mind: she suddenly understood where her name came from: her mother's friend, Evie. Perhaps that explains the disconnect between the two friends?

Several days later, Yoli visited Eva's parents. She entered a charming apartment built above a cliff and facing the sea along the coast of Netanya, the blue of sea and sky visible from every angle and infusing a sense of contiguity with nature, majesty, the infinite, of being surrounded by the massive universe.

Eva was surprised that her mother, Hannah-Yoli, chose to sit at the dining table away from the breeze. She was elegantly dressed, looking the way she would in healthier times: black sweater, pale yellow blouse with the collar raised. Eva was stunned. Her mother had spent much of the past year in a robe, sitting in her favorite armchair and hooked up to oxygen. Her mother even stood and greeted Eva and Yoli warmly. They were already feeling like two sisters on a joint journey to their mothers' lives. They sat on either side of her at the long table which Eva's father had designed and built to accommodate the whole family.

Eva's mother took Eva's and Yoli's hands in her own and pressed them to her heart, never letting them go for an instant. Eva's mother always had a firm grip and, despite her age, it remained strong.

"I never spoke about my childhood, my adolescence, my family," Hannah began, "or about life in the ghetto and how we came to Auschwitz. Perhaps, indeed, the time has come to tell the story. This meeting between the two of you seems so opportune.

"We were born to Hassidic families. They were very orthodox, but also openminded and modern. Yoli's mother, Rachel-Evie, was my age. We were very good friends from school but also because of our mothers. As was customary then, the mothers stayed home caring for the large families but both loved music, especially opera. I remember the beautiful dresses they would sew for us from the fabrics bought at your grandmother's store, Yoli, before the opening night of an opera. We'd go to concerts. On Shabbat we'd walk arm in arm along the city's main street.

"Cluj was a beautiful city and life for Jews there was, most of the time, good. We had Jewish schools, Jewish youth movements led by the World Mizrahi Organization. Girls and boys learned modern Hebrew, not just Biblical Hebrew. We loved going to the library to borrow books, especially those of Emile Zola. I particularly loved his book 'Nana.'

"At school I was always seated towards the back because I was tall. That way I wouldn't block a shorter child's line of vision. Or, perhaps, the teacher's to the children," mother smiled. "But Rachel-Evie sat in the front row because she was very short. It was the only time we weren't with each other. My father, Yekutiel, was an accountant for the city's Jewish hospital, as well as a ritual slaughterer. The hospital's reputation was renowned throughout Hungary because of its modern equipment, top-class doctors, and the research it produced. I was always amazed by the x-ray machine. My dream was to become a radiologist.

"When laws were declared against Hungary's Jews, everything changed overnight: the school was shut down; non-Jewish friends from homes around us were not allowed to play with us anymore; it became dangerous to walk along the boulevard and, of course, we weren't allowed in to see the operas and concerts. Your grandparents' financial situation, Yoli, became very dire. Luckily for us, my father was still needed at the hospital which served the city as a whole, not just Jews. That was our source of money for food, and my parents helped your family. Every day the restrictions got harsher, but we two friends still had each other and our parents did what they could to keep the mood at home positive. They also tried to keep us updated with schoolwork by bringing private tutors home, which also gave some income to the teachers who'd been fired from one day to the next and lost their entire livelihoods.

"Your family, Yoli, was one of the first sent to the ghetto. They were traders and the first round of new laws applied to anyone in business. With great sorrow we said our goodbyes, but my parents continued sneaking in food for them, as well as clothes and money, which helped sustain them, all things considered. We were among the last of the Jews round up and ordered into the ghetto, because of my father's job at the hospital. When your mother and I met again I remember how overjoyed we were, but I was shocked, too, because the situation in the ghetto was already terrible. We hadn't been aware of the degree of starvation, the lack of water. A framework was set up to try and keep the children learning, at least, but it was dreadfully difficult to maintain.

"One day my brother Moshe ran home happily, saying that an important-looking man, Dr. Kastner from Cluj, was encouraging children to tell their parents that a train would soon come to take them to a place where they'd find work. Of course everyone was thrilled because the ghetto had become insufferable. Our parents packed up small suitcases with essentials and arrived at the train platform. They hadn't expected the cattle cars; they were sure they'd board a regular train, the kind they'd taken when visiting their families in the Czech Republic, where my grandparents lived. Sometimes your mother would join me on those vacations," my mother smiled, looking at Yoli.

"Nazi soldiers on the platform urged us onto the cars, shoving more and more people in. Unlike others of Dr. Kastner's trains which indeed helped save some people, this train was earmarked for Auschwitz."

Hannah had reached the point where she always stopped. Now Eva hoped that her mother would expand on events occurring after she was separated from her family and until her arrival in the Land of Israel. When Eva read books about the Holocaust, and Auschwitz in particular, or other concentration camps which her mother alluded to having spent time in, she would ask her mother if she remembered this or that situation. Her mother's gaze back at her was always hollow and accompanied with a noncommittal comment like, "It doesn't matter, Eva. What matters is what we are doing now."

Eva thought back on her trip to Poland with one of her sons. Arriving in Auschwitz, they discovered that the only structure still locked and inaccessible to the public was the so-called laboratory where Mengele conducted experiments on living humans. From a document Eva read relating to reparations claims, she knew her mother had been in that building. Her mother was a strong, vital woman—independent. Only after reaching the age of seventy did life's tribulations begin to make themselves visible, primarily as physical difficulties, but she never let herself crumple in despair. Despite sarcopenia causing her body to shrink a good deal, she continued taking her walks, helped look after her great-grandchildren, and kept in touch with the grandchildren. She had a kind of sixth sense that let her catch every nuance in their voices or facial expressions.

Suddenly her mother stood, bringing Eva back to reality. "I need to rest. I've run out of air," she said.

"I'd like to ask one last question, if I may," Yoli said. "Did you see the young woman who gave birth to me?"

"Yes. Unmarried, pregnant young women were housed in a building where many young women arriving in Israel without families lodged. She was petite and her head was always covered in a scarf. She was very scared, panicked. But I don't remember more."

Eva and Yoli wanted to ask why the connection between the two good friends weakened, but decided to let it wait for the next time.

"Let your mother lie down for a bit," Eva's father said quietly. "Perhaps we just need to accept that we'll never understand everything and some questions will continue to echo inside us."

Yoli and Eva understood that their mothers were too hurt to overcome the events causing them to distance, and their solution to cease causing each other pain was to cease being in touch.

Does hiding a terrible secret help the psyche of the person hiding it? Is that true for every aspect of life? Eva wondered: can a family hiding secrets be considered a healthy family?

Yoli embraced Eva's mother briefly but warmly, wiped her tears away and gently kissed her mother on both cheeks. She and Eva left the apartment, shutting the door softly behind them, and headed for a café on the shore. A strong wind had whipped up and waves crashed fiercely.

"It's as though the air can feel the storm in our hearts," Eva smiled.

"You know," Yoli said, "I knew next to nothing about my mother's childhood, and certainly not about my father having a wife and children who perished in the Holocaust. But, as a child, I always realized something was being hidden from me."

"Oh, it's clear that my mother has some harsh memories which she isn't sharing with us," Eva added. They fell silent.

"Ever since I was a kid, my mother would say that women must remain independent and strong and that, if a man should attack you, kick him in his balls because it will make him double over in pain and give you time to run away." The two women laughed at Eva's mimicking her mother's manner of speech. "Do you think a statement like that coming from either of our mothers, without adding any explanation, is part of what shaped our lives? All the things that weren't said but from which you get the feeling that your family is harboring a secret? Even though they love you to bits: I wonder how influential those things are in shaping our lives."

Yoli nodded. "I once read a study on DNA and how non-biological aspects can definitely be embedded into who we are. Now I understand the study better. It seems some things are indeed absorbed, even if they aren't genetic, per se."

"Hmm. Having heard what your mother told you in your childhood, I remember mine saying similar things about independence and caution when it comes to men who are out to get you." They sighed, sorrow misting their eyes. Glancing up at each other, both simultaneously reach out to take the other's hand.

"I also understand how the secrets both our mothers hid not only shaped us, but our entire families, and how keeping all these things cloaked has seeped into our children's psyche. After all, every secret eventually comes to light in one or another way, directly or indirectly," Yoli said softly. "Do you think it's better to reveal these things only after the person keeping the secret passes away, when it's too late for questions to be answered, thereby avoiding confrontation?"

Yoli and Eva sat pondering. Neither had a definitive answer. "Probably,' Eva eventually said, "I guess it depends on the circumstances."

They were caught in a swirl of emotion, both feeling that the course was opening, closing and reopening old wounds, resurfacing matters that they'd suppressed or avoided, and presenting complex questions about forgiveness, the nature of being, the divine entity that only wants good for others, the concept that some people only see and live in their past, and justifying the past as the reason for everything happening in their lives.

"Luckily for us, our parents didn't let the past rule their lives, despite how harsh their pasts were and though the memories never go away," Eva said, then paused. "I think that Lesson 7, 'I see only the past,' can help us understand that we shouldn't allow the past to take over our lives because it lacks meaning, and only we imbue meaning into everything in our lives. On the other hand, it's hard for us to accept and implement this, which is why we oppose it so deeply."

"Maybe we can ask Avraham about Hitler, the horrors that

entire peoples endure, and how that aligns with forgiveness and containment," Yoli suggested.

"I asked my parents once," Eva recounted, "is it possible to forgive? My mother said no, but also yes. On one hand, it's nearly impossible to forgive the terrible cruelness she suffered, the loss of her family. It's so inhumane that it's hard to forgive humankind. But over the years she realized that the evils of one nation towards another doesn't encompass humanity as a whole. I think that if she hadn't come to that conclusion, she couldn't have been able to live a single day. My father, on the other hand, said that it's impossible to forgive, but he chooses to keep only the good memories foremost in his mind, like the owner of the kiosk in Vienna, a mother and her daughter. The kiosk was to be relocated to the forced labor camp. He remembers how that mother and daughter snuck an apple or a slice of bread to concentration camp prisoners and the Germans would pretend not to see. So within that environment of horrors he chooses to keep moments of humanity uppermost in his memories. He calls them the 'small miracles along the way.'"

"Do you think the entire Jewish race allowed itself to be terrorized?" Eva shared a troublesome thought with Yoli, one that also disturbed her in connection to her private life. "Does damage occur because you don't stand up enough for your own views? Because you're weak? Because you feel inferior? We now understand how deeply our childhood experiences can impact us, who we are, our ability to withstand hardships," Eva pondered aloud. "How important is our ability for self-love, both as individuals and as a nation?"

"I'm beginning to understand the book's statement that we are children of the Shekhinah, that we're in the image of the Shekhinah. When we love ourselves, we can also say 'no,'" Yoli replied.

"Yes," Eva agreed, "but where was that option when Jews

during the Holocaust were facing the crematoria burning them day and night?"

Yoli gripped Eva's hand harder.

"Our meeting... it's the first miracle that this course has brought us," Yoli said. "Who can even imagine what else awaits? Despite the complexity, I'm so grateful for having met your mother today. This encounter, for me, cleared up some of the uncertainty. I'm thinking that I won't open the adoption file. Today I realized how much joy I brought my parents and that I truly was the light in their lives, as they kept telling me. What remains unresolved for me, and I know for you too, is why our mothers decided to break contact. Maybe one day your mother will tell you. Maybe not. But at least we know how our souls are interlinked. The fact that you're named for my mother, and I for yours, is an eternal cosmic connection."

Their arms around each other's waists, they walked to their cars and promised to never lose touch. Perhaps that way their mothers' souls would still be together as long as the two daughters were in this physical world.

Slipping behind the wheel, Eva readied to pull out of the parking lot.

For some inexplicable reason, she began thinking of a particular instance when her husband had suggested taking one of his female employees with them to a wedding they'd been invited to. Eva wasn't thrilled with the idea. After a long day of work, and barely spending a second together for several days, she was looking forward to the drive home, which would allow them to catch up a bit. That time alone with him was something she sorely missed, especially in recent years after the children had grown up.

Actually, there were fewer and fewer such hours together. In retrospect, Eva had sensed a change already then. Now she remembered being annoyed at the employee tagging along, but her husband had explained that she had no other way of getting to their colleague's wedding because the employee's husband didn't want to join her. Eva agreed, as always, though reluctantly. It hadn't been the first time he'd brought along that same employee. Sometimes the employee's husband came too, even though Eva was not in favor of it, but she said nothing. She now asked herself: should I have insisted otherwise?

She decided to let go of her anger towards herself, towards the Eva of the past. Instead, she chose to acknowledge what she'd been through and embrace her new ability to recognize, assess, and understand when she must unequivocally stand up for herself.

Why was it that, after Yoli's meeting with her mother, these memories were surfacing? What was the connection? Was it, she wondered, linked to concealment and the way things are eventually revealed, even if we do our best to hide them? Sometimes, she realized, a memory floats up for no particular reason, nor does it seem linked to the particular time or place that it surfaced. She'd learned to simply accept that sometimes things could be illogical.

Chapter 6

"I invented the world I see."

Eva's phone beeped, waking her from a Shabbat afternoon nap. It showed 5 pm. Having not slept at all the previous night, she was happy to have caught up on a couple of hours. Her eyes half open, she made her way to the bathroom to freshen up, taking the phone with her. The message was from Odette, asking to meet her one morning for coffee. The message ended with two emojis: a heart and a smiley.

Eva felt herself opposing the idea for no apparent reason. Sometimes we meet people and can't explain what causes incompatibility or an instant connection. The idea bothered Eva, especially in light of the fact that the book consistently repeated how everyone was made in the image of God, how everyone was one, and how no encounter in life was purposeless even if it was uncomfortable, or painful, or made us feel bad. What hid behind her wish to evade and avoid meeting Odette? What deep hidden impulse lurked?

She didn't answer the message right away. She was going through a tough time, trying to pick up the shards of her soul, and wasn't really interested in any kind of in-depth tête-à-tête just now. But perhaps Odette needed a friend? She didn't want to reject Odette out of hand but she kept wavering between a positive or an evasive response. Avraham: she'd consult with him. Perhaps he'd guide her thinking towards finding the best way to handle the situation.

Avraham listened closely.

"Meet her for coffee," he said at last. His voice was warm and encouraging. "We can never know why we resist someone. It's like going someplace and feeling like a fish out of water, but we can't put a finger on why. Maybe meeting her will help you understand something that reflects your identity or resistance and is causing you the inner conflict."

Eva decided to take up Avraham's challenge. "I'd be happy to meet you," she messaged Odette back.

"I can't meet this week, I'm loaded with commitments, but can we make it for next week after class, when I'm supposed to tell my life story?" Odette's message pinged.

Eva was happy that there'd at least be a bit of time to wrap her mind around the idea.

Tuesday, 'the day of happy challenges,' as Eva called the day the group met, rolled around. Usually she was careful about working no longer than early afternoon, giving herself time to rest beforehand. Eva noticed that the weather on Tuesdays matched her mood. Or maybe it only seemed that way. She'd always known winter wasn't a season that made her happy. She suffered from the cold and, the colder it got, the slower she seemed to move. But from the course's beginning she felt as though she was influencing the weather: for example, when she cried, the day felt more humid. She knew this was a completely subjective sensation: but since the course began, the cold impacted her mood less, she was more accepting of it, and was able to function better.

Like longtime friends, the group's members were happy to reunite. Some had already formed connections outside of the sessions, aided by the group WhatsApp which Avraham set up. Now people shared all kinds of snippets with each other, thoughts that came up while at work or when practicing the exercises. People shared whether they found a certain idea difficult to absorb and some expressed their opposition to certain concepts in the book. The theory which caused the most common difficulty was one repeated in every chapter: that our thoughts create our lives and control us, such as the statement in Lesson 36: 'I invented the world I see.' Each group member carried with them life experiences they found difficult to contain, but they all understood that the declaration was fundamental to healing.

Avraham sat down facing the group, pleasant as always, gazing at each of them with his blue eyes, which always reminded Eva of her father's clear blue gaze. It was those light eyes and blond hair that had saved her father twice during the Holocaust: once as a young man in the German concentration camp, and later when he helped the Soviet military catch SS commanders. Were there perhaps, it now occurred to Eva, other instances which he hadn't talked about? Eva's mother always laughed when she talked about meeting a blond, blue-eyed chap and how, after being wounded during Israel's 1948 War of Independence, his hair was completely shorn and they returned a guy with light-brown hair. At least, she'd always laughed, she recognized him because he still had those same eyes.

Avraham, turning to smile in acknowledgment at Eva, asked Odette to begin.

Odette was a pleasant looking woman. Her face was round, her cheeks almost chubby, her hair black and curly. She wore wide black pants which, in Eva's opinion, weren't the most flattering. It was a little difficult to read Odette's facial expressions but she was clearly carrying deep pain behind the delicate, well-applied makeup. She also had a nervous giggle.

Odette had decided, unknowingly, to begin talking about her life from the moment she realized that her husband had a lover. And not just any lover, but a woman who worked in the successful company which she and her husband had established with their own two hands without any outside help.

"We both grew up in families that had things tough. We built a thriving company ourselves. We have three talented kids, all of whom have already left the house. None wanted to continue the company and, even though to us it was a pity, we accepted that they had different preferences.

"Our company focused on media advertising. We began to understand that something new was happening in this field which until then had primarily been based on written materials, radio and TV. Media and advertising were undergoing a change. So we hired an internet media consultant and caught the new trend at precisely the right time. It was clear we needed help. We interviewed several people and chose a very skilled young woman, a little too extroverted, blatantly so, in my view, with hair that was sometimes in shades of red, sometimes dyed blue around the face, huge colorful earrings, very tight tops, but mostly we were impressed by her organizational capabilities.

"That's exactly what we needed: someone to handle the pressures of our schedules from meetings to coordination with suppliers and clients. In the months after she joined the company I noticed the glances occasionally exchanged between her and my husband, but I simply banished the thoughts. They kept coming back and pecking at my brain like a woodpecker, but I was too busy with the company, which was developing quickly. Every evening my husband and I came home together, went together to conferences and conventions for digital content that were becoming more popular throughout the world, and I simply didn't let the pecker dig a hole, because I had a mission: our business.

"One evening, ten years ago, my worst fears came true. We came back from work together, as usual. We walk into the house and there at the entrance I see a huge suitcase. My husband simply said that he was leaving home. Just like that, without any prior conversation, without any preparation... "

Odette paused and took several breaths. When she continued, her voice trembled.

"It felt like a punch to the heart. I collapsed in a heap on the floor. I was sure a heart attack was next."

Avraham gazed at everyone, stopping once again at Eva, or so it seemed to her. Eva's heart shrunk. She didn't notice that two others, Emanuel, or Manu as he was called, and Tamra were feeling very uncomfortable and that Avraham hadn't looked just at her.

"That was ten years ago. We divorced a year later. But I keep reliving that moment as though it its occurring over and over. Since then I haven't had a life. I tried talking to him. I started therapy to try and understand what went wrong between us. Nothing helped. He wasn't prepared to engage in any conversation about the past. The only interaction we have is about work affairs, and only at the office."

She paused, as though experiencing it there and then. "Our friends used to be envious of us as a couple, of the way we worked together, always walked arm in arm, seemed to be so loving despite being together 'round the clock. I wondered if that's where the problem lay," she began to sob. "Our advertising agency was doing tremendously well. I'm the company's budget manager. My ex, which is still such a difficult word for me to say despite the years..." she sighed, "is the driving force behind the company, the one who visits clients, sits with them over business lunches and dinners, and markets our company to them.

"The irony is that I'm the one who brought this young woman for an interview with my ex, after being quite impressed by her at a women's group I was in back then. I was the one who recommended taking her even though she was quite young, fairly newly married with one little boy. Who could ever have imagined that she and the father of my children would stab me in the back? Yes, the father of my children. Perhaps that term is the easiest for me to use.

"What I find particularly difficult is that we're still managing the company together. It's the only job I know, it's my life, my meaning. No other advertising agency would take me on because the father of my children would immediately thwart any options, but it's what I know, I'm good at it, and our company is very profitable. It's also my only source of income.

"When we divorced," she was now sobbing more vocally, " I thought it'd be better if I were the one to leave, move somewhere else, and he should stay in the house. It never occurred to me, and no one thought of advising or cautioning me, that it'd hurt like the thrust of a dagger to see another woman moving into the house we built together with love, where every corner has a part of me invested in it."

Eva cringed in her chair, tears coming to her eyes. She wanted to hug Odette, to tell her she understands, but something held her back. How fortunate, she was thinking, that I said I wanted to stay in our home and didn't agree to leave, despite the sorrow that staying causes me.

"Stop for a second, Odette," Avraham intervened. "Take a deep breath." He walked over and placed his hand on her shoulder. Slowly her sobs subsided.

"All I'm asking," she continued, having regained her composure, "is for my life to carry on, but I can't do it. I get into a riptide of irrational thinking. I hate all men. Any man who tries to get close to me, I've got my poison darts at the ready. Now I only have female friends, all of whom are divorced like me."

Eva breathed in. In that instant she realized what was preventing her from connecting to Odette. Eva didn't hate all men because of her own experiences. She wanted to continue with her life; she didn't want to live in a state of depression, or let the split from her husband rule her life. On the other hand, Odette was an excellent reflection of where she did not want to be. Perhaps that could bridge a conversation or two. Maybe that kind of chat over coffee would be productive for both of them.

"I joined this group," Odette continued, "hoping it would give me the guts to leave the company, to forgive myself, and carry on with my life without grudges. My children are all adults seeking their own destinies abroad. Maybe they also fled."

Eva could really connect with Odette's pain.

"Reading Lesson 31, 'I am not the victim of the world I see,' I realized that's where I want to be. From my perspective, that would be such a release, a relief, just as the chapter says at its beginning: 'The world you see without, and the world you see within.' I really want to get to that point where I can look at everything that happened and tell myself that there's another way of seeing it."

"Is there a way in which we can help ourselves understand and accept that we're not the victim?" Avraham challenged the group, "that these are only circumstances which happened to us? Maybe as we practice and read together here we can tell ourselves, 'It's not in me, it's out there.' Maybe we can understand that we are children of the Shekhinah and the Shekhinah always wants the best for us, even if it doesn't appear that way to us. Could you read Lesson 35 for us? Note that it says: 'My mind is part of God's. I am holy.'"

Suddenly, from out of nowhere, Eva began singing 'The Days Ahead' in an undertone. She was surprised to find herself remembering the words to the song, especially since she'd never been much good at remembering lyrics and she was a terrible singer, always off key. She turned her head: Emily, sitting next to her and who hadn't said a word the entire session, had picked up the tune and was singing too, in a beautiful voice. The others gazed at her in amazement. Eva fell silent but Emily, her eyes shut, continued, not even noticing that she was now solo. And then at the chorus everyone, identifying deeply with the message, joined in, including Avraham.

As the group sang, Eva recalled the painting classes she'd taken with artist Adit Pank who'd penned the lyrics. How young they'd both been then, almost the same age, and both of them mothers to small children. Eva, not exactly a talented artist, had simply enjoyed being in the class, enjoyed its special energy, its freedom, which she hadn't found in any other activity. For Eva, Adit Pank was a brilliant artist with a sensitive eye. Eva's profession required such precision that these freely moving brush strokes in oils, not needing to be exact, being able to abstract an object such as parts of the body, to swipe with a palette knife, or even use her hands, spurred her wish to break free from the rigid frameworks. There in art classes she could express feelings that couldn't find expression in everyday life.

It was also the period in which she began buying healing crystals, sensing something beyond their exterior, and wanting to explore the unknown. Those were the years in which she felt unable to release what she was experiencing: every time she tried to talk about it, she sounded like an old witch practicing witchcraft. She always laughed when friends said that at least she's a good witch. But she remembered how her husband repeatedly mocked her. "You don't need to tell the world about the crystals you give the children. It's embarrassing."

Where had she hidden these suddenly surfacing memories? She remembered an earlier art teacher, a tall guy she found herself attracted to, physically and emotionally. She remembered being so alarmed at that realization that she not only instantly repressed it but, as a married woman, felt pangs of guilt for having such thoughts and feelings. She couldn't understand why she was reacting that way to him: after all, she was happily married. Wasn't she? Perhaps her marriage lacked emotion? Warmth? Art classes were a place where she could express and share feelings without belittling the knowledge she was gaining and without her husband tossing out comments like, "Do you think everyone's interested in all your nonsense?" What she suddenly remembered now was the sting of cringing inside but carrying on as though nothing had happened, doing her best not to make a fuss over his remarks.

The song came to an end. Emily opened her eyes and looked around, feeling embarrassed before she broke into a warm smile, perhaps realizing that by leading the song, she'd brought some relief to everyone.

Eva shook herself back into reality.

"Adit Pank, who wrote the lyrics, and passed away a few years ago, was my art teacher," Eva said. "She was an artist, a poet, a songwriter and, in later years, also delved into alternative medicine. Some of her paintings hang in my home. One, which I really love, depicts a railway line running off into the infinite, into the mist. There's an angelic figure in the background which, on one hand, is hazy, but on the other hand expresses heightened energy. The painting reflects my life and only now do I understood why, while gazing at it in the gallery eight years ago, I decided to buy it." Eva glanced momentarily at the group members before continuing. "Actually, everyone here is on that train leading into the unknown, into the fog. Only when the train ride ends can we see if our lives were on the right path."

People smiled attentively. The atmosphere in the room spoke of another barrier coming down. Only Emily continued smiling in her embarrassed way, wriggling about in her chair and switching her crossed legs. She didn't seem able to contain the moment and avoided direct eye contact with the others. Avraham gave her his comforting smile.

"I want us to carry out an exercise on fear," he said, "fear of the future as you sense it, because right now, Odette, you're feeling that the future is an unknown, and unknowns induce fear.

What exactly are we afraid of? As children of the Shekhinah, the Shekhinah is benevolent; it's our voice and, as we already learned, fear is nothing but our thoughts, not reality, as you've already internalized, or are in the process of internalizing."

"So, let's sit in a circle," he requested, "so that Odette feels us enveloping her just as the Shekhinah embraces us, not only at moments of distress and crisis, but also in the good times of our lives."

With Odette in the center and everyone surrounding her, Avraham spoke directly to her. "Try to tell yourself and us what could happen if you decided to inform the father of your children that you are leaving the business partnership for the purpose of continuing your life, and releasing yourself and him from this mutual commitment."

Odette's face showed pure terror. Her eyes reflected a mix of anger, or fear, that only someone who's been in such a situation could catch. She was too scared to look into anyone's eyes, fearful of seeing a reaction that she didn't want to see.

"Release him?" she hissed. "To take him into consideration?"

"Releasing him," Avraham said gently, "is for your own sake. It frees you from being chained to oppressive thoughts. You're the one who won't have to see him and his new partner every day. You're the one who won't need to be present at company events when she's hosting in the home that was yours. How does that sound?"

Odette's eyes began to sparkle, this time not because of tears, but at the thought of the emotional and conscious freedom she'd attain.

"So... I'd be without work, without an income, but with way too much time to think about what happened. That would make me even more withdrawn."

"And what's happening right now?" Avraham persisted. "How does your life look right now? Are you free? Are you having a great time? Do you sleep well? Without sleeping pills?"

Odette drew in a deep breath, and another, and yet another.

"Let's all take in some air, hold it inside, and then release it in one go as we scream," Avraham suggested.

At his signal, breaths were audibly drawn in. And then, at his signal, a great shout came from the circle, causing the Bridge teacher on the lower floor to race upstairs in worry, barge the door open, and stand there feeling a bit foolish as the group gazed at him, smiling.

"Now I want to understand," Avraham said, "why you wouldn't have an income? Sure, you won't necessarily have that monthly salary, but you have a pension, you are worth half the company's value, you have your own apartment without the constraints of a mortgage, you have your own car, a new one in fact, which I noticed when we entered the parking lot at the same time before this class," he smiled.

Odette seemed to have calmed down somewhat.

"Do you understand that all the complications are in your own head? We are familiar with our own past. We're living the present as we speak. And the future? We'd do well to keep underlining the concept that we are the sum of our thoughts, and I apologize for repeatedly reminding you all of that."

Avraham went back to the sentence that Manu had begun reading when the session commenced. "The way we see ourselves is how our ego perceives us. We don't view ourselves from the perspective of sanctity. We experience ourselves from the perspective of what the ego is comfortable seeing. Ego controls our fears, blames us for various situations, even though the reality is very different. The reality we perceive ourselves in is an illusion. Fear drives us, causes us to be helpless, panicked, incapable of understanding that our intellect is part of the Shekhinah's intellect, and as such it's sacred."

Avraham studied Odette, then gazed at each of us in turn, and asked how each person was feeling. Most were relieved.

Eva could feel that moment of sanctity. She couldn't explain to herself what that exactly meant but she could sense a comfort when she thought about the possibility of staring fear in the eyes and understanding that everything was the result of thoughts.

"A certain degree of fear is beneficial to us," Avraham explained. "It's a primordial fear that makes us run if we see a lion, or jump aside when a car is coming towards us. That type of fear drives our physical survival instinct. It's the only type of fear that we need to be familiar with."

Turning to Odette again, Avraham asked: "What do you need to do, at the practical level, in order to release yourself from the chains tying you down?"

Odette thought before answering. "Discreetly meet with a lawyer and accountant and estimate what the half company is worth. I have all the company accounts." A moment later she stood and went over to Avraham, hugging him.

"It'll take me some time to implement. I can't do this overnight, but thinking about it has already calmed me." She paused. "I read ahead in the book but only now I'm starting to understand the title of Lesson 42, 'God is my strength. Vision is his gift.' Until I sat here with you all and told my story as I experienced it in my own thoughts, I couldn't comprehend any of the book's statements. Everything sounded like an interesting collection of ideas or philosophies, but what did they have to do with me? I wasn't really willing to even try and understand."

Studying Odette, Eva suddenly wanted to undo Odette's ponytail, which didn't allow a single strand of hair to escape. To Eva, that too-tight hair style symbolized Odette's constraints, the past and present so tightly intertwined that the future couldn't find a way to set itself free.

The class over, Avraham's homework was the regular request: to read the next few chapters.

The group members straggled out. Eva caught up with Odette near the stairs outside.

"Can I ask you a question, Odette? A personal one?"

"Sure."

"How old are you?"

"Fifty-five."

"We're the exact same age!"

Odette's face showed surprise. Eva wore skinny jeans, a tank top with a short-sleeved shirt thrown on top, shiny red sandals with white dots, and the whole look was young and easygoing.

"How's that possible? I was sure you're at least ten years younger than me!" Odette exclaimed.

Eva smiled. "In addition to some good genes that I guess work in my favor, I'll tell you something else. Got a minute?"

"Sure. Am I rushing anywhere? No. I don't feel at all compelled to get back to the computer at work and actually work!"

The spring evening was pleasant, the air even a little chilly, stars sparkled and Eva reached into her car, offering Odette a shawl for her shoulders. Shawls had become an inseparable part of Eva's look after her trip to India. She remembered going into a shop in Varanasi's market and feeling as though she'd stepped into Ali Baba's cave. Thousands of shawls in every color imaginable were piled on shelves from floor to ceiling. The richness had taken her breath away. She left the store with twenty new scarves—some for very cold weather, some for light breezes, some as elegant accessories, some for everyday use.

She wrapped herself in one, too.

"Come on," and tilted her head, "there's a nice café right across the road. Let's get a cappuccino and a fresh croissant and have a chat. On me."

Finding a quiet spot on the deck, they gave their orders to the smiling waiter. Both were in a great mood after this class even though it had been intense. Although the meeting had focused on Odette, Eva also felt swaddled by the blanket of supreme sanctity when the group had enveloped Odette.

Both hands wrapped around her mug, Eva took small sips,

carefully choosing words which she hoped would inspire Odette towards finding her path to release.

"Up until not so long ago I dressed like you, Odette. Suits, elegant attire, well-put together. Jeans? The thought never crossed my mind. Tank top? Over my dead body! No one should see my cleavage, even a fraction, at a business meeting. Most of my work is with men on construction sites. I supervise projects. When I went out with my children's father to formal events, he wanted me to look classy, not flirtatious. To add value to the business. I was always envious of the women who took to the dance floor with abandon, who let go. But that was so far from who I was. That just wasn't me." Eva paused, then smiled warmly. "Only later did I realize that it actually was me!

"And then the day came when my husband left the house. I remember staring at my wardrobe. I emptied it. In a fury, I threw everything in a heap on the floor in the center of our ample walk-in closet covered in mirrors. Everything. Bras. Underwear. Nothing was left on the shelves. Then I took a deep breath. 'Okay, Eva,' I told myself, 'you're young, slim, in great shape, your husband's left, and it's time for a change.' I sat down on this pile of clothes which, as you can imagine, were quite costly, and cried my heart out. I picked up each item of clothing, remembering where I'd worn it, and why. I cringed inside when I recalled all the events when someone had complimented my appearance, and the only one who never did was my husband."

Eva paused again, taking a couple of sips of coffee.

"A few months before my moment of truth we were in Italy. I stepped into the Versace store, having seen the prettiest dress in the window and wanted to try it on. The sales assistant sized me up and took the dress to the fitting room, which was lined in black velvet and accessorized in a yellow-gold tone. One wall held a large mirror with the Versace lion emblem. The dress fit perfectly: it was a sexy piece that spoke of mischief, and definitely not the kind of thing I would ever buy. But it looked so good on me. I stepped out of the fitting room in elegant black shoes that the assistant had brought to complete the look. I was beaming.

"My husband studied me and what do you think he said? 'You've put on a bit of weight. I don't think this dress works for you. It's too tight and revealing.' That was a dagger in my heart. Yes, I'd put on maybe three kilos, from a size 38 I was now a 40, but his comment took the wind out of my sails. The sales assistant didn't understand what was going on. He saw me step out feeling fabulous, feminine and, in an instant, the balloon popped. I went back into the fitting room, slipped off the dress, put it back on its hanger, glanced at it one last time and left the shop without saying a word, still longing for that dress. I decided to get rid of the excess weight and, on the next trip, I'd buy the dress."

Odette listened closely to Eva's tale. The breeze loosened a few stray hairs: quickly Odette tucked them back into place with a clip.

"A few days later," Eva continued, her cup almost empty, "I was driving my husband to work. I pulled into parking lot and another car also came to a halt. One of the women employees, whose body was, shall we say, full, stepped out. I knew her well. She'd been working at my husband's firm for twenty years. I turned to glance at my husband.

'Wow, she's quite plump,' I said, smiling.

'Really? I never noticed,' he answered."

Eva's gaze concentrated on Odette's eyes.

"What I couldn't figure was this: how is it he notices I'm up three kilos and claims I'm getting fatter but, when someone else in his daily environment gains weight, he doesn't notice? But you know how things are: you brush it off and then totally forget the whole thing.

"I did buy that dress a few months later. I found it amongst the pile of clothes on the floor and a memory flashed in my mind of that encounter in the parking lot. I stood, put most of the clothes into the empty part of the wardrobe where my husband's clothes had been. That was one of the toughest things after he left: opening the doors and seeing empty shelves. I canceled my meetings for that day and went shopping.

"Jeans. One pair. Another. A third. T-shirts with low necks. G-string underwear." Eva chuckled. "Well, I ended up leaving most unopened in the drawer because they were such a nuisance, creeping up when I walked. I couldn't for the life of me understand why anyone thought them to be comfortable! But I bought some sexy bikini underwear with matching bras, some tops that are thin enough for the bra to be just barely perceptible and which go well with a blazer I had that I love. I didn't give up all my blazers. I couldn't. I do need to look presentable at business meetings.

"And then there was that special moment when I went to a cosmetics store and, in an act of daring, tried on fire red lipstick. I remember a young guy walking past, really good-looking, who smiled at me and said something about how the color suited me. You can't believe how those few words affected me. For too many years no one had noticed my appearance and, what was even more painful, I wasn't paying attention to it in the right way, either. I was always the pretty little girl, and then the pretty young woman, and so on. I always dressed in the way people expected me to. It's odd how pretty little girls sense everyone assessing them by their beauty. Me, on the other hand... I always felt transparent, not of the 'just be quiet and smile' kind but more like 'you're invisible,' you aren't even here.

"From senior high on, I began to express my opinion, but in a gentle manner. For years afterwards, a childhood friend said I looked inaccessible, introverted, even elitist, aloof. That shocked me. Defining my image was motherhood, my husband, my career. In retrospect, that mode of dress was convenient.

Only after trying the Versace on did I realize how, inside, a part of me was raring for freedom. In my business life, it was clear to me that things needed to stay the way they were. But that dress... it was a formative experience. It taught me what self-love actually means, how much I'd put my own needs aside, how much I'd canceled my own presence.

"I decided to meet up with Shira, a friend who did manicures, and made an urgent appointment. During that period she couldn't get why she needed to repair my nails almost every week because they were coming apart. I always had strong healthy nails but I knew exactly why they'd weakened, I knew my mental state was having a direct influence on my physical state of health. I just didn't have the courage to tell her the details. But one day I phoned her, and happily for me she was free right then.

"I turned up at her house and told her that I wanted to share a secret, and make a request. A brief overview of the crisis at home, without too much detail, and she understood everything.

'And what's the request?' she asked once I'd regained my composure.

'I want you to paint my nails fire-engine red.' Her eyes flew open. Until then I'd always used a neutral delicate pink, or gray, or palest blue. 'The color that expresses the burning in my heart,' I explained.

"She just smiled. I trusted her. I knew she could keep the secret. We had a really good relationship. Sometimes she also told me about her difficulties at home, her wish to go out and have some fun, whereas her husband was a homebody. We laughed and decided to go out together, maybe even overseas. We found a fun café on the Caesarea beachfront and decided to adopt it as 'our place,' somewhere we could share heart-to-hearts. We also had our regular table. I even remember the waiter seeing us coming one time and calling us over with a grin, saying our spot was waiting. But we never did go abroad together. Shira was diagnosed with cancer and, from that point on, navigating the treatments became the focus of her life. So the dream to travel together was never fulfilled.

"But that day, I left with bright red lipstick, bright red nails, tight jeans that hid sexy lace underwear, a thin white top that showed a bit of cleavage, and felt like I could take on the world. The next day I showed up for a meeting with the engineers and consultants of a large project I was working on armed to the teeth with skinny jeans, open sandals, a bright orange top with a V neck, a lightly padded bra and, of course, my nails and lipstick. There was that moment of shocked silence, everyone looking at the unfamiliar me, but I took my place calmly at the table, more confident than ever and, in a clear voice, presented the project to the contractors. In that instant I realized that the way I'm perceived depends entirely on what I convey. Partway through the meeting, I felt what we're learning about now: that I'm the child of the Shekhinah. I just didn't know how to formulate it into words back then."

Odette smiled warmly. As they stood to leave a gust of wind loosened the clip in Odette's hair, freeing it. Her hair came tumbling down: a cascade of gorgeous curls. Pulling strands out of her face, Odette smiled. She didn't even bend to pick up the clip. On the contrary: she untangled the clip, tossed it away, bent over, ran her fingers through her hair to shake out the curls, then stood, flinging her hair back in one go. To Eva it seemed that Odette's whole body, not just her mouth, was smiling. Laughing, they walked to their cars.

On the drive home, Eva's mind was busy. She remembered Emily's voice and wondered about what had freed her enough to allow her to sing in front of the group. Recently, one of her acquaintances had commented on how she'd changed. "No," she'd answered, "I just let myself be me for the first time in my life."

She wondered: what happens when our true voices break

through? There's a lot of common ground between Odette and me but, on the other hand, a huge difference, too. Eva simply wasn't willing to capitulate to the stormy waves battering at her life, dragging her into states of mind where she sometimes felt she could barely come up for air.

There was a point when she got so low, she wondered what point there was in continuing to live after realizing that all her husband's promises were nothing but a charade. That day she had phoned him and, from the background sounds, it was clear he wasn't at an office meeting as he'd said. She herself had been on her way to an important meeting that would close a company's decision to sign her onto a large-scale project. That job would keep her busy for a good while.

But, on the way, she'd passed a small hotel on the outskirts of Herzliya, and saw her husband's car was parked there. In a flash she saw the whole picture. Her heart raced. The phone rang. She was thrilled when the client apologized and asked to reschedule. Her day now freed up, she let the storm in her heart get the better of her and put her foot down hard on the gas and just drove, fast. Luckily, her excellent reflexes saved her from crashing into a lamp post. Deep down, she didn't really want to end her life.

She pulled over and took some slow, deep breaths, drove to a seafront in Tel Aviv that she knew would likely have very few people, and simply did a disappearing act for the rest of the day, not answering calls or being where she was meant to be. Parked as close to the shore as she could be, she gazed at the horizon on that wintry day, the winds whipping up waves that crashed on the rocks. A few surfers who loved that kind of weather were out enjoying themselves. Rain smashed against the windscreen in perfect timing with her tears.

Sitting there, she wondered what might happen if she simply walked into the water and disappeared forever. She sat like that for hours, letting the phone ring: her husband, who called several times, and then her therapist, probably alerted by her husband. That kind of behavior was very unlike her. Even when in extremely important meetings, she would at least text back quickly that she was busy. This time... nothing.

And yet, the idea of disappearing from the world scared her. She found it incomprehensible: how could she, an accomplished architect, a doting mother, a loving grandmother, even arrive at such thoughts? She sat in the car for hours, crying over the knots that had formed in her stomach in and the fear of what lay ahead.

Eventually she headed for home. As a red light was about to turn green, the car next to hers tooted and a voice called out, "Hey? How are you? Long time no see!" Eva gave a thumbs up and a forced smile, and drove on.

That car horn was like a wakeup alarm. She had to find a way to not get bogged down and become melancholy. She must carry on despite the difficulties, as her therapist kept telling her. "You'll learn to cover up the wound. Occasionally it might reopen and sting a bit, but the more time passes, the shorter the healing time each time it does open."

Eva thought about Avraham's assurance that they'd each reach a stage of forgiving. How she longed for that, mostly towards herself. She walked into her house and she threw herself onto the bed but couldn't fall asleep. It was as though her body was digesting the turnabout in her life. It made her uncomfortable.

Shadow barked furiously. Eva reached for the baton her father had given her long ago when she'd had to travel alone. After her husband's departure, she kept it near her bed. She made her way downstairs glancing around and switching on the outdoor lights surrounding the house. Nothing seemed remiss. She went back to bed, her heart pounding, wondering whether she should nonetheless call her husband who'd promised that if she needed him, he'd be there for her.

Then the house alarm started bellowing. She'd never felt so afraid. The security call center phoned; she asked them to come out and check. Meanwhile, she got her courage up and walked around the house, finding the door to the living room slightly ajar. She mentioned this to the security guards but they found nothing. She knew it was impossible for the door to have been left open. The guards said they'd wait for a while longer.

Another wakeup call, this alarm going off, Eva thought. She must not let fear control her.

Yet her body trembled. She decided to call her husband. Had she expected him to uphold his promise?

"I'm afraid," she told him, explaining what had happened.

He snorted. "So what do you expect me to do? Cope with it," he said and hung up. She collapsed into a pool of uncontrollable tears, the kind she hadn't given in to since the actual split. On the kitchen floor, her phone in hand, she wept. Shadow snuggled his nose up against her, licking her cheeks. What a slap in the face! A shockwave: he really couldn't give a damn about her.

Other alarm bells went off over the years but Eva chose not to see and not to hear: now that they echoed in her mind, she she's they were practically thrust in her face. Glances that weren't directed at her. Slight touches between her husband and his new partner that might appear random but which she realized were loaded with significance.

There was that company event they'd attended at a luxurious villa. The main room was comfortably full, there was great music, people splashing around in the pool. So was her husband. Surrounded by women employees. And one lay on her back, held gently afloat by his hand. The sight shocked her so much that she couldn't make sense of it. She decided to leave and talk to him later, reproach him for not behaving appropriately with the women employees. Then, too, her eyes had seen. Her brain had opted not to compute.

It was becoming clear: the time had come for her to open

up, to receive support not just from her children, her sister and sister-in-law, but to confide in others close to her, just as she'd shared with Shira. Eva realized she was starting to digest what her therapist had been saying for a year: she wasn't to blame. The situation had nothing to do with her personality. Or, as she put it, "Even if you'd been standing naked in the kitchen with a wooden spoon in one hand and a broom in the other, telling him about your great meetings that day, he wouldn't have noticed."

That image made Eva smile.

She wondered if there was really such a thing as unconditional love. Could such a love be achieved, as the book promises? Could a true believer, no matter what religion, experience pure love?

Look at me, she thought. Fifty-three. Married twice. Sporadic relationships in between. Certain her relationships were supportive and loving, but perhaps she'd never experienced real love.

Can unconditional love last through a long couplehood? Does boundless love exist, the kind where one is ready to die for the other, the kind touted in movies? Can one experience a love which is more powerful than anything else? One in which you get as much as you give, and what you receive fills your soul? Is there a love where disputes are resolved with a unique gaze that brings two people back to the realization that their love is cardinal and where they most want to be, and where they feel protected?

She knows that she is blessed and the love for her children, her grandchildren and her parents is exceptional. Even if arguments occasionally arise, they get beyond them. But she's also realistic enough to understand that not every family has that level of love for one another. When she volunteered for the night hotline, she would hear stories of domestic abuse, harsh situations and flagrant disrespect which clearly attested to an absence of unconditional love. Where might she find that kind of love, then, for herself? Slowly the lessons began to seep in: everything that happens in life is part of a divine plan leading to life's goodness. Can true love, in harmony with Shekhinah, exist? Unconditional love?

Eva stood. The marble floor was making her chilly. Looking around, she stroked Shadow's head and the dog happily returned to sleep. That night, Eva's grandfather came to her in her dream. He had been a rabbi and she'd been privileged to have had his active involvement in her life until she was twenty. He smiled, his kind eyes crinkling at the corners as he whispered to her, "Don't worry. You'll be fine. You're strong. You'll have some hard days, but I'm watching over you."

The ringing phone wakened her: a good friend with whom she'd begun sharing her experiences just calling to say good morning. Working together for many years, he could hear in her voice that Eva was in distress. Without sharing the details, she did say she was experiencing a couples crisis.

"I'll talk to you later," she'd said on that fateful day.

He interjected before she could end the call, "You haven't forgotten that we have to go through some project details, right?"

"Sure, sure."

"What do you say we arrive an hour earlier and find a café where we can sit and you can tell me a bit of what's going on with you? I know how it was when I was going through a divorce a few years ago... maybe I can help you think things through."

With a sense of relief, Eva had agreed. In the wonderful warmth of a streaming shower to start her day, she realized the day was not far off when she'd have to disclose the truth to those close to her, especially her parents, because these things couldn't stay hidden for long. She'd lost so much weight that people were asking if she was ill. Evasion had worked only so far, until someone had actually said, "Eva, your smiling eyes haven't smiled for a long time." Yes, she knew her eyes were sad these days.

Her parents: she dreaded the thought of telling them what she was undergoing the past thirty months. Tears fell from her eyes. They'd loved her husband, treated him like a son, and now she'd have to tell them about their upcoming divorce.

Lesson 323 came to Eva's mind.

"Here is the only 'sacrifice' [...] to give up all suffering, all sense of loss and sadness, all anxiety and doubt, and freely let your love come streaming in to his awareness, healing him of pain, and giving him your own eternal joy..." And as we pay the debt we owe to truth – a debt that merely is the letting go of self-deceptions and of images we worshipped falsely – truth returns to us in wholeness and in joy. We are deceived no longer. Love has now returned to our awareness. And we are at peace again, for fear has gone and only love remains."

These statements refine the questions I've been asking myself, Eva thought; in the next session I'll ask Avraham if that's even possible.

CHAPTER 7

"I merely follow, for I would not lead."

A day before the next meeting, Eva read the statement on leadership, thinking about how it related to her. Do we really follow a predetermined destiny? Is my role written in stone? Can I divert from my preset path to the degree where I completely break from it? A bit like navigation software, she thought. But mostly, why is a reroute, followed by the understanding that this isn't my intended path, accompanied by so much pain?

At the next meeting she shared these thoughts with the group. Avraham, moving his chair to sit across from her, noticed tears in her eyes. His penetrating gaze was clearly catching something which she still wasn't aware of.

"So can you see that whatever you did until now was like the promo for your life? Actually, you need to be sitting here in my place, Eva. Now, let's meditate, which might reveal some insights to each of you relative to the statement Eva shared."

Thoughts still swirling in her mind, Eva immersed herself in the meditation. She loved her profession. Architecture and design offered a plethora of linked activities. She thought of them as a basket of wonderful produce, the truffles of life. Her vocation encompasses aesthetics, always important to her and possibly influenced by her home life as a child, her father a furniture draftsman and her mother an expert seamstress who made all the girls' clothes, often ahead of their time in color combinations and styles. Her profession was one of colorfulness, imagination, daring, research and learning, and human interactions. As far as her career was concerned, she felt she was definitely in the right place, and happy with it.

A year before her life turned upside down, she had begun to feel that she'd reached the maximum she could as an architect and was ready to consider new directions. She dreamt of setting up a place to bring parents and children from disadvantaged regions together with those of more privilege areas towards promoting greater acceptance and integration. The concept was to give the poorer children a springboard into a better future and provide the children from more well-to-do homes a chance to actually help by forming connections and providing support for their peers. She wanted to name the center 'Tomihali.' The plan was to establish it together with her daughter.

But when her life crashed she abandoned the idea, becoming emotionally unavailable. More correctly, she deferred it, promising herself that when her life was back on stable ground, the center would be founded, but possibly in a different format. One thing was eminently clear to her before the breakup: she needed a change. She never imagined the scope of that change, the amount of energy she would need to deal with the breakup, her family, her work environment, and how her pace of life would take an about-face.

Avraham is most likely right, Eva reasoned. There's a message in the statement: 'Your loving Voice will always call me back, and guide my feet aright.' Maybe I woke up at the perfect moment in the course of my life; with two cute grandkids, three of her four children already settled down with partners, having completed their studies and now working in jobs they enjoyed, and her youngest in military service. The nest had emptied and now she was free to give herself some care.

For days Eva had searched for a pivotal moment, perhaps one she'd been completely unaware of at the time, when she felt alone in the relationship despite having a full life. She scrabbled around, one image after another, until she eventually pinpointed where and when.

She was sitting in the lobby of Kaplan Hospital's surgical wing, a gray and gloomy place, where the lack of investment in anything to lift people's moods as they waited for those double doors to swing open with preferably good news, was blatant. The lobby held simple chairs with cushioned seats that had completely flattened over the years, without armrests. No TV, no newspapers, nothing. Only people, focusing inward, worry and fear for the wellbeing of their loved one showing on their faces. Nothing there should have distracted her. Even the walls were painted a simple white, bare of paintings or wall-hangings. There was no coffee corner or snacks wagon albeit everyone there was too afraid to leave for fear of missing that important moment when the surgeons would come out with an update.

She'd sat there alone. One of her sons, injured during army duty, was undergoing a second, highly complex surgery on his hand. Before he was brought into the operating theater, she'd stopped the surgeon for a moment, begging him. "Please, just make sure he can continue his work on the computer and play the piano."

"I'll do my best," the surgeon answered.

Eva's husband was at the office. "There's no point in both of us just sitting there. Call me when the operation's over," he'd said.

The swinging doors opened and shut, again and again. When they did, those in the lobby could hear the beeps of medical devices. In and out they went: doctors, nurses, dressed in green, dressed in blue, dressed in white, some with colorful headscarves; another surgery concluded, another, and another. And she was still there, alone. Eva suddenly fathomed how incredibly alone she'd been there. No good friend calling to ask how things were going. No one offering to come and sit with her for a while. Her husband occupied in his office instead of holding her hand.

Three nerve-wracking hours later, when Eva was on the verge of tears because she had no idea how things were progressing, having exhausted herself pacing back and forth in the small lobby which was now almost completely empty, the door hinges creaked yet again, and out came the surgeon, grinning.

"Didn't I make you a promise? I worked on his hand as though it was Lego. I built it all back up like new," he said, hugging Eva as she burst into sobs of relief. "Don't worry," he added softly, "it'll be fine." He glanced around. "Where's that young man's Dad? What... are you here alone?"

"Yes," Eva answered as a nurse stepped out. "Your son's asking for his mother," the nurse smiled. Thanking them, Eva followed the nurse to the recovery room, embraced her son, sat next to him, and stroked his head the way she'd done when he was a little boy. He was still very much under the influence of anesthesia.

"You'll be okay," she said, perhaps unconsciously reassuring them both. "I'm here, you'll be fine."

When was she able, she called and update her parents, knowing how tense they'd also been. Then she called her husband.

It took six months from the time her son was injured until Eva felt she could breathe freely again as she watched her son regaining his hand's capabilities. Throughout those months the family had rallied to help. Eva stayed home much of the time, except for a few brief work meetings that she couldn't reschedule. When she did have to go out, another of Eva's sons stayed at home. Eva was fully invested in her son's process of recovery. Her husband, busy with work commitments, helped in the mornings and evenings.

Yet Eva continued to feel terribly alone the whole time. She found the lack of friends who could be a source of support and comfort highly stressful: no one suggesting she take an hour off to meet them at a café, no one calling to see if they could take her place for an hour to give her a breather, no one taking an interest in her son's recuperation.

The project managers Eva coordinated with knew about her situation and did their best to make things easier. They made sure she was given feedback on problems, including reports and photos, and they were the only ones to consistently inquire how her son was doing. She'd only found out later that several friends had actually called her husband, who simply said his son's recovery is progressing.

Perhaps that's where the breakdown began, with the sharp realization of the absence of a circle of friends. Recalling that period, Eva's heart broke as she wondered why she didn't share more, ask for help, say that she needed support, discard the veil of elegant clothing as well as the external image of resilience and invulnerability. That's when everything cracked, peeled, and began to dissipate, she realized.

Now, in the meditation session, she thought about the many times she waived her own needs or wishes. She thought about true friendships that she no longer had, about the decision to take all the guilt on herself. Despite being opinionated and strong, she closed herself from the world outside and still couldn't understand why she'd done that. Maybe the coming lessons would allow her to delve deeper and find the missing pieces of that puzzle.

Avraham spoke, drawing her attention. "My friends, I don't feel too well. I came thinking whatever it was might pass but I need to bring this session to a close now. My apologies."

Eva went to the kitchenette, returning with a glass of water for him. People slowly stood. Emily went over to Avraham, letting him lean on her as they slowly walked to the elevator. She then accompanied him to his car, made sure he felt well enough to drive, and returned to the room, advising everyone that at least he was able to do that. Nonetheless the group members were worried. It was disturbing to see their strong group leader suffering and unwell. No one spoke. They just nodded goodbyes, got into their cars, and drove off.

Eva was as concerned as any of them. His state reflected in his eyes. The WhatsApp group quickly filled with get-well messages.

"Thanks, everyone," Avraham answered. "Perhaps work stress got to me, but I promise we'll be fine for the next meeting."

CHAPTER 8

"I have given what I see all the meaning it has for me."

By the next meeting Avraham was looking great again, smiling broadly, arriving a little ahead of time and joining the others in the kitchen.

"So what's the cake on today's agenda?" he laughed.

As always at the start of a meeting, he first gazed into each person's eyes. When asked about this amazing ability, he explained that it comes with practice and that everyone can achieve it.

Only some years later, when Eva learned ThetaHealing, did she understand how it was possible to communicate with or check on someone else's well-being, even from a distance.

"Before meditation," Avraham said, "we'll start this meeting with an exercise to help us work on the chapter's opening statement. Let's pair up, facing each other, and do a two-minute round. Hold hands and look into each other's eyes."

It was awkward. Eva could feel her palm breaking into a sweat.

"Try to clear any thoughts you have as you watch the other person. Just be present in this activity," Avraham requested. "It's not easy, I know. Thoughts keep racing around, our eyes want to break their hold, feeling embarrassed, but make the effort nonetheless."

Initially almost everyone smiled. It took about a minute before a more serious tone took over and people were able to concentrate.

"You're thinking about how hard this is," Avraham said, "but at one of our coming meetings we'll do this for a full five minutes while seated facing each other."

That brought to Eva's mind a mantra that her daughter had taught her: Sat Nam, Sanskrit for 'I am truth, truth is inside me.' Every time her thoughts badgered, she thought of it.

The exercise over, Avraham began a twenty-minute meditation session. It was the first time that Sharon, who always came a few minutes late, began the session with the others. At every meeting Avraham had increased the length of the meditation. Eva now felt more confident with the experience, and that Avraham's direct gaze into her eyes at the opening of each class made meditation so much easier. Her greatest difficulty was remaining seated on the straight-backed chair. This time Avraham suggested that anyone who might be more comfortable lying down could take a mattress from the pile in the corner and do so. He knew them well enough by now to be sure none would actually fall asleep.

Eva bunched her coat into a pillow before lying down. The topic of this meeting was healed relationships. The group's members listened to Avraham's instructions with their eyes closed.

"Imagine yourselves at this moment standing in front of someone you find difficult to forgive. What is the nature of the contract between you?" he asked, giving them time to connect to the concept and process the experience.

In the silence, the group members withdrew into themselves. A stifled sound of sobbing came from the opposite corner of the room, and then long breaths of release.

Back on their chairs, Eva spoke. "Honest? I have no clue how this contact looks, what it contains, what its foundation is. Is it between me and myself? Between me and someone who hurt me? And what's the essential difference between relationships that are sick and those that have healed?"

"I think," Nathan responded, "that sick relationships are founded on fear and healed relationships on love."

"And should we wait until we feel whole in order to reach the stage of recovery?" Avraham asked.

The question was left hanging.

"Time for something tasty," he gestured towards the kitchen. Ginger tea, coffee, delicious pastries, a chocolate cake and an orange cake baked by Sharon and Emily, who had clearly been discovered as the group's best bakers, and lively conversation on the session's topic.

"When do we feel whole? What drives the moment when we recruit everything we've got in order to heal, to recover the relationship, whether inside ourselves or between us and someone else? Is the moment we can feel love towards anyone we come across also a moment of release? Does the understanding that we aren't putting the blame on someone else, and that we carry the blame, lead us to freedom?"

The consensus was that they still had a long way to go before they reached that point, and everyone was still troubled and had difficulty understanding the idea that for a relationship to heal, responsibility and blame must be assumed.

Slowly the group members made their way back into the room, questions whirling in their thoughts. Although she understood the process in principle, Eva knew she'd have trouble accepting the idea. They took their seats. Avraham gazed at each of them.

Nathan asked the group if he could speak. In most meetings, he tended to listen, occasionally adding a scientific explanation and presenting details from research, especially when it came to communication between distanced human brains, brain biology, and various studies which aimed to understand the human brain's functioning. An academic, a year ago he'd decided to take a break. Tall, pleasant natured, of kind eyes, he loved telling jokes. On the other hand, he was very tough on himself. Every so often he claimed that he didn't understand how he got to the course, he of all people who, so he claimed, was as far from things spiritual as the sun from the moon, and spent his life immersed in facts.

"I'd like to talk about addiction," he began.

Immediately, Eva felt uncomfortable. The first association that came to mind was drug or alcohol abuse although neither seemed to match Nathan's personality. But her work with the help line for sexually abused women had taught her that appearances could be extremely deceiving, nor do they indicate what a person's innermost being truly holds or is capable of doing.

"I'm here because I was trying to understand, as I said in one of the meetings, why I can't seem to lose the weight that is so disruptive to my life. I'm intelligent..." he smiled sheepishly, "and I've come down with all kinds of illnesses that clearly are linked to obesity. I dream of the day I can bend over and see my shoelaces. I dream of the day I'll stop puffing after every minor exertion. Even here, the short walk up one flight of stairs leaves me so breathless that I take the elevator and watch you all racing up the stairs like it's nobody's business.

"I married very young," he continued, a slight undertone of bitterness, or perhaps apology, in his voice. "Life at home was challenging. I was always the chubby kid. An excellent student, yes, surrounded by friends at school, but I could never bring them home even though we had a spacious, even luxurious, house in a prestigious suburb in central Israel.

"My father was a despot. A very smart businessman, sought after by local tycoons. My mother was beautiful. She completed her studies in law and even sat for the bar exam but never worked in her profession or, in fact, anything at all. No self-realization. She came from a less affluent home than my dad's.

They met in the army. He'd show up with his fancy convertible, very rare in Israel and certainly not driven by a nineteen year old soldier. My mother was serving on a base located in central Israel and wasn't required to sleep there. Most of the people serving there were incredibly smart, or had the right connections to get in there. I think it was the previous iteration of what is today's 8200 signal intelligence unit.

"My father had studied in England in an exclusive boarding school. Being distanced from his family and friends at such a formative age influenced his personality in harsh ways, or so that's my hunch. He grew up feeling he was better than anyone else around him. He was always very generous towards other businessman and politicians, wanting to be in their good books, and he was financially generous to our family, but only for appearances' sake. Within our four walls, he controlled us with an iron fist. We couldn't do a thing without him okaying it. We had to learn how to play an instrument: mine, the violin and my sister's, the piano, so that he could proudly laud us to his guests as we gave recitals. He bought my sister the most expensive Steinway in the world. He bought me a Stradivarius for which he paid at the time half a million dollars.

"We were required to study additional languages. My sister was forced into ballet classes and hated every minute of it. At least once a month she affected a high temperature on ballet day. Of course, none of the best physicians around could find a reason for her, ah, malaise, let's call it. I was required to become an excellent competitive swimmer. And all that was so my father could tell everyone what talented children he had. It goes without saying that grades under ninety were utterly unacceptable. It was very fortunate that we were smart, that we enjoyed most of our studies, and could do well in exams with very little effort.

"My mother did what she could to soften the sharp edges of my father's demands but, all in all, she too was under his tyrannical rule. To all intents and purposes, she had it all: money, clothes from the best designers in the world, trips abroad on a private jet, get-togethers and meetings with the who's who locally and overseas. In photos you always see her smiling, a glass of wine or cocktail in her hand, but we saw how our father gripped her elbow, and how our mother's eyes never smiled. They constantly conveyed terror.

"Every so often a bluish bruise would show on my mother's arm but it was always, 'Oh, I slipped on the stairs again.' I do remember that when my father was in the house he would order her around, tell her to phone and book a place at some restaurant for a meal with his friends, for instance. Obedient, she carried out the orders smoothly and immediately. She did have opportunities to go out with her friends in the daytime but had to be home before he came back.

"My mother was extremely intelligent. She tried to envelope us with warmth, but wasn't very successful. My father's cruelty towards her simply locked her heart up. As a boy, I didn't want my friends to see my father's attitude towards her or see his anger attacks at me and my sister. They came out of nowhere. We never knew what the trigger was, which is why I didn't want friends to come over.

"At my grandparents' home, my mother always acted as though everything was fine. We loved going to my mother's parents. It was the only place where we could be hugged and loved unconditionally. I don't know if they sensed what was happening to my mother. They passed away when I was an adolescent and I never had the guts to talk to them about life at home.

"When a few friends did ever visit at home, it was always when my father was abroad. They were envious of my huge room, the luxury, the furniture from the most expensive stores, the food we'd order from the best restaurants, our frequent trips overseas. I could never tell them the truth, not even my closest friends. They said I was just a snob who didn't want them to see my amazing life. And I just smiled, super annoyed inside.

"I think one of my high school teachers caught on. She called me in one day for a conversation and asked how my mother is, and whether I'm happy. I did tell her a bit of what was happening, but it seems that in the next conversation with my father at a school meeting, when she tried to say something, or ask, or allude to the situation with him, he so dazzled her, as he did everyone, that the matter was simply set aside.

"At the first meeting in my army unit once I finished basic training, there was a girl who I thought was so charming, so warm, and I just fell in love. Head over heels. She came from a very different background from mine: a warm, loving home, very demanding when it came to studies but the relationship between her parents was really good. Or at least, so I thought. Very quickly I proposed. Money was never a problem for me. My grandfather left me a monthly income that equated to a living salary without ever having to work, but we were both keen to continue our studies and immersed ourselves in our careers. Her parents felt fortunate that their daughter had married so well, into a wealthy and well-known family. Of course their family received me warmly.

"What surprised me was that my parents didn't oppose the marriage. My father told everyone about his daughter-in-law's father who'd been wealthy in Iraq before coming to Israel, and how he'd have to leave everything behind and start from scratch here.

"Later I began to think that perhaps it was easier for my mother that I wasn't home. My sister was also about to enlist. Maybe my mother thought that with both of us out of the house, there'd be less tension and she'd suffer less. I guess I'll never know.

"It was important for my parents that we have a great big flashy wedding. My bride was appropriately impressed by all this lavishness. In our first years, while we were still studying, we were very happy. We supported each other, which wasn't too problematic because there were no financial hardships. But to my astonishment, when our first child was born, I found myself married to a woman who started behaving like my father. Let's say that the money had gone to her head. I wanted to continue in academia, but that wasn't enough for her. She wanted more and began demeaning me in front of our child.

"Meanwhile, our second child was born, a sweet little girl, and my wife preferred to bring in an au pair, adopting mannerisms of wealth that were foreign to me. She abandoned her career as a human resources manager in a large hi-tech company. The only thing that interested her was travel abroad, clothes, jewelry.

"This wasn't the warm, wonderful woman I'd fallen in love with. She mocked me in front of friends for my choice of an academic career, told me I'm no more than a zero, that I'm not a success which is why it's convenient for me to study, lecture and hide away in my research laboratory which, by the way, was about to reach a breakthrough in a biological field that would have been a revolution in biological pest control. When I tried explaining about the articles I was writing, or the global scientific publications, she was so derisive. 'Why do you think all this nonsense interests anyone?' she'd jibe."

Hearing those words, Eva shivered and tears gathered in the corners of her eyes. The countless times that her husband had shut her up with that very statement! Mocking her feminist opinions, her knowledge in various fields. "Why do you think it interests anyone?" he'd taunt. Instantly Eva would shut down and cringe inside.

"My life turned into hell," Nathan continued. "Suddenly I found myself living my mother's life! There was constant fear over what set my wife off. My children, who are my greatest love, started mimicking her approach. They stopped telling me what was going on in their lives. Not only did I no longer have any say in what happened to them, I had no clue what was happening in their lives.

"That's how I started to binge. Drown my sorrows in food. Get fatter, eat in frustration over getting fatter, then do it again, a vicious cycle. My growing weight was accompanied, of course, by more nastiness, and my wife's harsh statement that she was ashamed to be seen with me in public. I sunk deeper and deeper and couldn't see a way out of it all. I didn't want to divorce. I pitied the children, but their attitude towards me was the hardest thing to take.

"The turning point came when I was invited by a New York university to lecture. I met a friend there, a colleague, who was shocked to see my huge size. On the final day of the conference, after successfully delivering a talk on one of my discoveries in the biological laboratory, we sat together at a pub.

"He studied me. 'Spill...' is all he said. 'You're not getting on the flight back until you tell me what's going on.' It was clear to him that I was going through a terrible period. We knew each other from our earliest university studies, and he was one of the few people who I'd told about my childhood.

"We sat there for a few hours. I wept over my bitter lot in life, blaming my wife for all the ills, shedding tears mostly over the difficulties regarding the children, who are more precious to me than anything but for whom I basically no longer exist.

"My friend stared at me. And kept staring at me. 'You do understand that you're addicted to being wretched, right?' he eventually said. I stared back in shock with tears falling from my eyes. 'What do you mean by addicted? How can you be addicted to wretchedness? Addiction is to alcohol, food, drugs, but to misery?' Yet he persisted. 'Look at yourself, look at your life story. In childhood you were miserable and friends didn't come to your home. You fled your home. And here you are now, miserable again, blaming your wife, crying over your children's attitude towards you.

"And where are you in this whole story? Where's the clever boy who can withstand his father and support his mother? Remember that time you told me about the day your mother once again 'slipped on the stairs' and you went to your father? You were only sixteen and barely taller than him. You told him that if you ever see your mother slip again, you'll make sure he slips far harder and it won't end with just a black eye... remember that? You came to my house in a total panic and told me what you'd just done, standing up to your Dad despite the fear. You were so proud of yourself,' he said."

Nathan paused, shaking his head as he recollected that event.

"My friend stared straight at me, then reminded me of the story's pivot. 'You told me,' he said, 'that you copped a whopping slap on the face from your dad, and it was the most fantastic slap you'd ever received because, from that day on, your mother never 'slipped' again. So where's that man now?

'Instead, you're sitting here sobbing over your miserable fate because your wife acts towards you the way your father behaved towards your mother. See? You're addicted to being wretched and miserable. That's the only way you can face the truth: by not being honest with yourself. Think about it: what are you trying to flee from? All this excess weight is just a massive cover-up for a soul that's screaming for help!' he said to me."

Nathan stopped, took a deep breath, and looked at a note he was holding with a text he'd written down.

"My grievances hide the light of the world from myself," he read.

And suddenly in one go, sobs that had been bottled up for months, if not years, seemed to explode from this large man.

"My goal in coming here," he sobbed, "was to heal my soul, to start a new life after managing, at least, to divorce. Because of that conversation in New York, I boarded my flight holding a small paperback with a red cover which my friend gave me. It described all kinds of addictions. I landed, went home, and told my wife that we're divorcing. I kissed my children, both of whom were in their late teens, and said that I'd always be there for them, but I can't stay here a minute longer. Then I packed a bag and left the house.

"My wife was in total shock but she didn't oppose the divorce, which went ahead quickly. I left her the lavish home, generous child support, and money for her own life moving ahead. I live in a charming home now and it's all mine. For the first time in my life, no one stylized my surroundings for me, I didn't hire any renowned designer or architect, because all I wanted was to wander the shops and choose what I loved.

"I started rediscovering myself, but I still didn't lose any weight. I think that's because a sense of guilt is still bogged there, deep inside, and I can't get to the bottom of it. Maybe I feel guilty over not helping my mother in her distress, or not telling my grandparents, or her sister, because maybe they could've helped her. My mother ended up dying fairly young from thyroid cancer. It's clear to me now that her cries for freedom were stuck there in her throat, thereby manifesting that illness. When she fell ill my father, as always, made sure the best of doctors were around but did he sit at her side? Hold her hand? Offer her support? Nothing. He hired nurses 'round the clock and that absolved him of having to care for her himself.

"Maybe I'm still putting on weight because I'm angry at myself for not having been alert enough to how the relationship with my wife was developing. I can't help thinking that, had I been paying attention, things might have been vastly different. Somewhere inside I still love her. She was my first girlfriend. Any couples-related experience I had in my lifetime was shared with her. Despite the difficulties, I never cheated on her.

"In all that chaos, though, there's a point of light, because my children have reinstated their connection with me, maybe because of the fact that I stood up for myself and walked out, which made them see me differently; maybe as being brave rather than pitiful, someone who decided to take up the reins of his own life again."

Nathan drew in a deep breath. His tears were accompanied by heaving sobs.

"Let's take a few minutes' break before we continue," Avraham suggested. People reached for bottles of water under their chairs, or stood, stretched, and walked around a little. Nathan remained seated, trying to restore calmer breathing. Odette brought him a glass of tea, the kind she knew he liked. He smiled and nodded in acknowledgment.

Going to lie down on a mat in the corner of the room, Eva thought about her life. Does the couple relationship we choose define us? Does the crisis we experience define us? After going through this process of completion and recovery, will I be able to redefine who I am?

She was feeling vulnerable: a woman whose life had been shaken up hard. Everything that defined her had been undermined. Her career was also impacted. She lacked the patience needed for clients. For the first time in her career, she made a mistake when planning the renovation of a law office's reception area in an exclusive office block. The office had invested a great deal in planning, but she'd nevertheless made a critical error. She absorbed the cost of course and, within days, the carpenter had the new reception counter ready, but the damage to her reputation wasn't easy to restore. At least, that's what she presumed.

We can have a years-long career with zero mishaps, and then one screw-up and bam! Everything gets turned upside down. That's how Eva was feeling: everything she'd built had collapsed in an instant.

She stood and returned to her chair. Most of the group was back, cradling cups of tea.

"All I want," Sarai said, "is to convey the sense of love to you, and hope that you can understand there's no point in thinking over and over about where you went wrong. I'm sure your mother is looking down on you with love, and thanks you for standing up to your father with such heroism."

"We can be angry at ourselves as children," Yoli continued, "but we need to embrace the child that we were and forgive ourselves."

Avraham smiled at what he was hearing, them quoting his own explanations.

"I'm glad that you're starting to see the significance of unconditional love for the child inside, that you're understanding the statements 'My redemption comes from me' and 'Forgiveness is the key to happiness.' In the end, if we forgive the child within us or our adult selves, we can continue on the path to our own redemption, which is where the key to happiness lies. The basis for sacred relationships is firstly the connection to ourselves. In general," Avraham explained, "everything starts with love and with the connection to my inner self. The unique interpersonal relationships, with a partner, between colleagues at work, between parents and children, are based on six stages:

- **Stage 1:** I'm not okay.
- **Stage 2:** I need to look for a partner who'll hide the guilt.
- **Stage 3:** The honeymoon, creating the special contract.
- **Stage 4:** Breaching the contract.
- **Stage 5:** Negotiation in an attempt to restore the contract to its former status.
- **Stage 6:** Separation and creating a new contract.

"Sacred relationships which are authentic and healthy," Avraham added, "and which, by the way, are never fully upheld, only occur when we are linked to our self and our unconscious essence."

Avraham looked at each of the group members. "I want you to focus this coming week on thinking about these six stages relative to yourselves and your friends, your partners, your work, your parents and your children. Try to examine which of the six stages you're at, specifically from your place of difficulty. Write about it. Bring this place to the next group meeting."

The session over, people went downstairs to the parking lot, including Nathan, who'd decided to make the first step towards a physical change which would accompany his psychic change. Nathan walked alongside Eva.

"I think I've still got that book I spoke about. Would you like to read it?"

Eva didn't understand why he was offering it to her but didn't want to insult him.

"Sure, I'd be happy to," she answered.

He walked to his still very new car and opened the trunk.

"Maybe the mess in here reflects where I am in life," he apologized sheepishly. "I promise that the next time I open this up, it'll be organized. Not to impress you, but for my own sake."

The red booklet was beneath a pile of professional books. Nathan handed it to her with a comical ceremonial bow, as though handing her a treasure. Smiling, Eva thanked him and curtsied.

"You know, Avraham was right. Those sandals of yours with their shiny black straps and little white spots, along with the nail polish on your toes, should be banned in public, and certainly not allowed on a woman as lovely as yourself."

Eva kissed him on the cheek in thanks for his compliment.

At home, she hoped that the book might shed some light on how she was feeling. Following Nathan's descriptions, she began thinking of types of addiction. Maybe some people really are addicted to the detrimental aspects of their lives. Maybe they do that to justify some element in their past since that place, although hurtful, is familiar and known. That thought shocked her: was she also living that way, which is why she can't shake herself free? She hoped to find a sliver of insight as she glanced at the book.

Eva slipped into bed. After her husband left, she rearranged and restyled the bedroom. She didn't want anything to remain as it was: she repositioned the bed, bought new linens and even a new mattress.

Putting the book down next to her, she fell asleep right away, not having had the strength to read even a single page. It stayed there the entire night.

In the morning Eva felt more motivated. She'd slept well and without any disruptive dreams, which rarely happened in the past few years. Generally she woke every night feeling choked by dreams of being chased. She knew what the dreams meant and found dealing with that very difficult. Nonetheless, when the idea of sleeping pills came up, Eva rejected it. It was a period when, alone at home, she feared losing control, remembering the time she'd taken a quarter of a pill on a flight to the States because everyone said it would help sleep through the whole flight, but she woke with a migraine that took two days to overcome.

Without a doubt, I fear losing control, Eva confirmed to herself. Nor had she ever drunk more than a small glass of wine. Her greatest fear was surgery requiring full anesthesia. The idea that things were happening around her but she had no control over them frightened her. She feared waking after surgery and having no concept of what had occurred during those hours. The fear worsened when she realized that during surgery her eyes might open, but see nothing: no clues, no words, no discomfort. It was a state of complete loss of control over her life.

The week passed quickly. Eva read Nathan's book. Each page brought her additional insights. The words penetrated like pushpins in a corkboard. Each word stabbed her to the point of physical pain. It was so tangible. So frightening. Rereading some sections, Eva realized that she, too, was addicted: to discomfort, to fear, to life being turned upside down. It was a tough thought to cope with but she decided that, each day of the week, she'd write several brief sentences about her suffering to see how it might be serving her in her current situation.

Taking a page, she marked three columns. In the first, she'd record the event. For example, 'I was cheated on.' In the next she'd write how she felt afterwards: 'insulted' in this case. The third column would list what she might do, as of tomorrow, to try and feel the opposite of insulted, some small action that would lead her to feeling, for example, brave. Maybe going to a film alone. A silly thing, but she didn't have the courage to do that. For her it was a pitiable sight to be seen there alone.

The cinema nearby was showing a movie she really wanted to see, about the life of Edith Piaf, but who would she go with? Friends and acquaintances had recommended it to her. 'La Vie en Rose,' it was titled: a rosy life. Piaf's life was anything but rosy. Eva checked where else the movie was playing and chose one in an area where she knew no one. Not bumping into anyone she knew would at least make her less self-conscious about being alone. This was her alone-baptism.

Bit by bit she realized that her situation wasn't that different from Nathan's, which may be why he offered her the book.

Despite being very busy with the new project, Eva decided to sit every day and devote time to writing at least one line summarizing her feelings. She was going to delve into the book's content, no matter how hard it had hit her in the gut.

CHAPTER 9

"My grievances hide the light of the world in me."

Eva arrived late and very upset to the next meeting, barely able to maneuver into a parking spot and almost hitting the car next to her, which was the kind of thing that never happened to her. She was an excellent driver: she knew that had she not been, it may have prevented her from spending so many hours on the road. Now she sat in the car, hyperventilating, sweat dripping down her back. That, too, was something that never happened to her.

She worked at breathing slowly, but felt nauseous: was this an anxiety attack? When she'd calmed down a little, she stepped out of the car and headed indoors, barely able to make it up the stairs. From outside the door she realized that Avraham had already begun the meditation session.

She knocked softly, knowing that Avraham did not like when people entering during meditation. But Avraham noticed that she was on the verge of collapse. He ran to the door and signaled to enter quietly, supporting her gently. Eva sat, her eyes swollen from crying. Avraham gazed into her soul. Her breaths were sharp but she tried to join the meditation session.

As soon as it was over, Eva burst into uncontrollable sobs that she never knew were bottled up inside. Her body trembled. The group members were taken by surprise. Avraham brought her water, placed his palm on her forehead and slowly calmed her. Between sobs, she told them what had brought on her reaction.

"I phoned my husband. We recently separated for a trial period, but we're in touch. He promised he'd be alone during this time so that we could focus on how we feel as a couple. Anyhow, I phoned to tell him I was going out to the class and I'd call again when it was over. 'No problem,' he said and that he'd be working late because he needed to prepare material for the board meeting tomorrow. So I got into my car and set out.

"As always, I had classical music playing. Ravel's Bolero, this time. I was approaching the junction before the turn to the city, and I see his car signaling for a right turn. I was stunned. No more than a minute earlier he'd said he was in the office, and his offices aren't anywhere near that junction. I braked suddenly. The car behind me almost crashed into mine. Without thinking twice I phoned him. I was holding on to a shred of hope that I'd made a mistake, misidentified the car, the driver, that he'd pick up and say he'd call back because he was in a meeting. He didn't answer. The music seemed to get louder and louder in pace with my increasing heartbeat. A sharp pang of pain flashed through my temples.

"I decided to tail him. He made the right turn, me following. He turned into the parking area of an apartment building and I went in too. And then his passenger door opened and a woman I know stepped out. That's when I realized she's his lover, and that he'd broken the promise not to meet with her. Although he'd already left the house, the therapist we were seeing recommended that he try not meeting his mistress so that we could rethink things and reach a mutual decision about our relationship without the fireworks at home."

Eva dabbed at her eyes and nose with a tissue. "He never promised, but I'd hoped he'd at least give it a try. A second later he saw me park facing him. The woman quickly got back in the car and they raced away. I tried taking photos, I don't even know why, because I know who she is, but I couldn't really do much because I was paralyzed, my hands shook, I trembled uncontrollably. And the whole time, Ravel kept building up to his crescendo, heightening the tension, as though someone at my favorite radio station was purposely matching the music to my heartbeats. I don't know how I managed to get my hands on the steering wheel, turn the car around and drive here. My husband phoned and phoned, over and over, but I didn't answer."

Eva shook the entire time that she spoke. Avraham couldn't begin the class. He knew who was slated to talk today and the background to the woman's story but wondered how to go about this unexpected change to his plan. Before he managed to pull his thoughts together and say anything, Emily walked over to Eva and sat down facing her. Emily, who since the course's start had barely uttered a word, sat quietly, listening. Emily, of whom no one in the group knew very much beyond the fact that she had a very sweet singing voice and was always happy to share quality chocolates or her delicious cakes. Emily, who always wore gray or black, never a color, and never wore sparkly jewelry.

"I want to ask your forgiveness," Emily said, placing a hand gently on Eva's shoulder.

It seemed that the world had come to a stop and ceased turning on its axis; as the Bible verse states: "Sun stand still in Givon, and the moon in the valley of Ayalon." No one breathed. The tension was so thick it could have been cut with a knife. Only the sounds of a bird chirping and a mewling cat outside could be heard.

Eva's eyes, staring at Emily, showed terror, and perhaps even loathing. Could she be one of the women Eva's husband had cheated on her with at some point over the years? Avraham stood next to Eva, realizing that a chaotic scenario could develop. Eva appeared to be on the verge of fainting.

"I don't know your husband," Emily said softly, almost

inaudibly, "but I'm the 'other woman' having an affair with a married man I love."

A sigh of relief came from everyone, even though it was clear now that Emily's story wasn't going to be an easy one to hear. Emily returned to her place. Even though it was Sarai's turn to share, an exchange of glances between Sarai and Avraham gave him the okay to ask Emily if wished to speak today.

Emily took a deep breath and began.

"I was married for about twenty years. Were I to show you photos of me during that period, you wouldn't believe it's the same Emily. My hair was crewcut, not because I didn't love my long, brunette hair prior to marrying, but because my ex-partner or, more correctly my ex-husband, because he hardly saw himself as being in partnership with me, didn't want me to be attractive. He didn't want the outside world being drawn to me.

"My marriage was violent but, make no mistake: not physical violence. He never raised a hand to me. Only recently I realized that I lived under horrific emotional terror and abuse. And when I reached this realization, after years of kowtowing and trying to please everyone in my world, I decided to simply up and leave. One day I came home from work and asked for a divorce.

"I was amazed that he agreed immediately, without even opposition. After the divorce was finalized I began to comprehend how powerful the abuse had been. I have three fabulous kids who fill me with strength. For their sakes, I held up during that period of sheer terror, probably because I also didn't believe I was worth anything much. I didn't believe I was pretty or attractive, smart, funny, or capable in any way.

"I admit here openly that even today, as I say these words, five years after divorcing, deep down I still don't believe I'm any of those things. In my innermost heart I'm still worthless; at most, a very low-level office worker for some unimportant business at a workplace where I'll never be able to show my strengths. I don't have a degree but I have a triple doctorate in life.

"And nonetheless, I keep thinking that without academic qualifications I'm worthless because that's what my husband made me feel all those years. 'I saved you from being a nothing, so you owe me,' he'd say repeatedly. And to prove that he saved me, he'd go through my phone, follow me around, insist I report who I'd spoken to and where I'd been. I worked with the public, which made things worse. I was living a nightmare my entire marriage. I was too scared to leave the job because, after all, who'd take me? On the other hand, my job was my escape, a place where I was appreciated.

"And then there was that moment when I felt I just couldn't live in that atmosphere of strangulation anymore, with a husband whose had total control over my every move, including who to choose as friends, how to deal with the kids, even which car I could drive. I was so afraid to get into that car lest I move or alter anything: not the seat, not the mirror, not leave behind any indication of the car somehow belonging to me.

"Outwardly, I lived a good life. There was no shortage of money. We lived in a private home with a garden. But I never dared buy myself any item of value because that might make someone envious or draw attention to myself and, anyhow, I didn't deserve anything nice or valuable.

"The moment of release: whew, I can't even begin to tell you how that felt. I decided to move out and let him stay in the house. Suddenly I could breathe again, I could drive wherever and whenever I wanted, I could negotiate the world in my way. My first decision was to never cut my hair again. I let it grow way below my shoulders. For the first time since marrying I could talk to people without fearing I'd be criticized in front of them, or in front of the kids, or at home.

"The next decision was to look for a different job. I still couldn't imagine myself in anything beyond a menial position, but a friend suggested I interview in a place that admittedly was male dominated, dull, but it was a change and, no less importantly, the salary was a bit higher. It was clear to me that I needed to earn my own livelihood. I took a mortgage to buy a home, managed the expenses: things I'd never handled before.

"Initially the workday passed pleasantly enough. Slowly compliments were voiced by the owner. A word here, an admiring gaze there. I was very flattered that a man was paying attention to me simply because I was worthy, and I knew I didn't have to fear anyone's reaction.

"From words and light caresses, the situation moved to actions. He told me that things weren't good at home and that I'm the most amazing woman in the world. You can't imagine what this did to me. It sent shivers of joy into my soul. It released my sexuality, made me dizzy with excitement, made me feel I did have worth, that I was feminine. A man coveted me—it made my mind and heart spin.

"I tried not to think of the fact that the man had a wife and children at home. Maybe things like this really do happen in real life, not just the movies and, if he's having such a hard time and I'm the woman of his dreams, he'll leave his home and family and we'll live together happily ever after. Not only that, but he was affluent and the thought of a man like that being attracted to me, wanting me, making me feel that I was worth something, totally overwhelmed me. I felt like a queen. On top of the world.

"And yet, in the back of my mind, a thought niggled. Like a bird whispering that I'm doing a bad thing, I left a situation that constantly quashed me and entered a place that embraced me as a woman, but I was once again living a lie, lying to myself and the world. Especially tough for me: facing the kids, my parents. I was part of a couple, but it was all top secret, clandestine, never to be mentioned in public. Sure, I've got happiness, but it's all locked up in a cage.

"And then Passover or our New Year or some other Jewish festival comes around and, once again, I'm alone. It used to be that I was alone in the marriage, and now I'm alone despite being in love with a man who admires me. I imagine him with his family, kissing his wife, sleeping with her in their bed. Those are very tough images to deal with. My life has not made a 180 degree turn. I'm living a new reality, but still pretending. I started rethinking my life, where I'm at, living a lie, being in that status again.

"What was going on? I kept asking myself. I tried talking to him a few times, asking him if he loved me and if he'd really leave his family. But he always evaded a true answer. 'Sure,' he'd say, 'but not right now. The kids. The business. You know. And I'd be hurting my children's mother.' Slowly my patience ran out. Didn't I deserve more? I asked myself. I need to spread my wings, the ones I wanted to believe I had.

"But mine weren't the brilliant colors of peacock wings. Mine were the peahen's, nothing but gray. No color. Nothing that would draw anyone's attention. Yes, I had long beautiful hair, I dressed well, no one was interrogating me, but I was more alone than I'd been before and this type of alone was no easier.

"Then one day his wife came to the office. I was sure she gave me knowing glances. I shriveled inside, said that I wasn't feeling well, and left. I didn't come to work for the next few days. He called, trying to understand what caused me to flee like that, but I didn't answer. That was the moment I realized I needed help. I could see I'd been trapped in this state for years yet nothing had changed or would change. I don't even remember who told me about this course, but at the end of the year I decided that the whole affair needed to be put to sleep, so I registered.

"I'm not the kind of person who opens up easily. Maybe living in the kind of relationship I did locked my insides up. I don't know, but one thing was clear: I couldn't carry on that way. I don't yet have the guts to leave and he keeps asking me, begging, not to go. When he looks at me I melt inside and we go on like before but, inside, I can sense, and know, that it isn't the right thing for me.

"Eva's been through a crisis of betrayal. The truth is that as soon as that became clear, I thought of leaving the course. How could I look her in the eyes and tell her my story when I know that I'm a woman who wrecks families. Even if it doesn't lead to divorce, it's sabotage, its cowardice, it's a betrayal of trust."

Throughout almost the entire time that she spoke, Emily hardly glanced at Eva who sat hunched over, trembling at times. She also noticed Manu hunkered down in his chair, fidgeting every so often.

"Every lesson I experienced here," Emily continued, "is a revelation for me. From Lesson 85, 'My grievances hide the light of the world in me' and 'My redemption comes from me' I've started to see that the grievances I felt in my heart towards my husband seep into what I feel towards my lover, and especially towards myself. I'm in the dark, and my actions hide the light from me. I decided that I want to see beyond the cloud encompassing me and realize that self-grudge, or grudges towards others, won't light my peacock feathers from inside."

Avraham asked Emily to read the chapter aloud. When she read the sentence, "Today I will recognize where my salvation is. It is in me because its Source is there," Emily stops reading. It's her turn to burst into tears.

Eva is very embarrassed. The situation is uncomfortable, as is the flood of emotions she experiences. She's not meant to feel compassion towards a woman who's done what Emily has. And yet compassion is flooding her. What does that say about the 'other woman'? Does she not deserve love? Emily came from such a turbulent marriage, and now someone cares about her. She experiences that caring as love. Is it really forbidden?

Eva quickly shakes those thoughts off. The situation angers her. She is angry with Emily for making her feel that way.

Neither of the women feel a sense of relief. Both are showing deep distress.

Avraham catches the situation's fragility but, at the same time, it also creates a special connection.

"Let's take a break," he suggests. "I think we all need a bit of an emotional and physical pause. Coffee, something sweet, a slice of Emily's cake. All helpful," he adds, smiling.

Emily offers Eva a slice of cake. Eva can't bear to touch it, even though it's her favorite: cheesecake. Eva feels like she's choking. She can't explain the flow of emotions running through her. She studies Emily through a different lens. Suddenly she begins to catch on to the shades of black and gray that Emily constantly wears. It comes from inside, from feeling she must never stand out because, in Emily's perception, she's a gray and black peahen. She's even managed to choose a shade of gray that doesn't highlight her eyes and delicate beauty.

Compassion mingled with terrible fury. On one hand, she wanted to understand but, on the other, her vulnerable state made that virtually impossible. And yet she found it hard to begrudge Emily. Grudges, Eva knew, would undermine her plan for self-redemption, for release from the situation and its outcomes. Her head turned toward Emily, sitting off to one side and surrounded by other group members, supporting her, embracing her even, and felt anger towards all the compassion she was receiving.

How do I go on from here? she asked herself. How do I get to a point where I can talk civilly to Emily? And about what? Maybe this is an opportunity to understand what could drive a woman to become 'the other,' the second fiddle who is constantly put to the side, the one who, bottom line, still ends up alone at night, or on festivals and holidays, who goes alone to functions, who doesn't go to movies or theater or even to cafés or restaurants with the person she loves and who claims to love her.

It seemed to Eva that two different entities were seated, one on either shoulder, one saying this, one saying that. Yes, this meeting was highly emotionally charged for Eva, who entered it from her own low point, but also for Emily who decided, at last, to expose her narrative. But the meeting also held a formative moment where both women, on diametrically opposed sides of the situation, realized that nothing is black or white and that there are countless shades of gray in between. Perhaps the time's come, Eva thought, to put aside what we think are our feelings and truths, which have directed our lives even if they're incorrect.

Both Emily's and Eva's thoughts went back to the early classes in an attempt to understand the concept that a chair is a chair because that's what they were taught. Everything and everyone we experience in our lives builds us, layer by layer, until our perceptions of who we are takes shape: work, studies, teachers, partners, all of whom make our truths 'present' and designates a place for them. These are the symbols we're taught to use as guidelines, as explained by Don Miguel Ruiz in his books The Four Agreements: A Practical Guide to Personal Freedom and later, The Fifth Agreement, which are meant to reveal the source of self-limiting beliefs that rob us of joy and create needless suffering.

Eva nodded. It's so hard to see beyond our circumstances. It's so hard to see reality, and also what our realities conceal from us: that there isn't one single truth, or even two or three. Every truth attained in life comes from the culture in which we live, from what our parents have taught us, what our environment conveys. We stumble in the dark, which is not so much a physical darkness as an emotional one.

Lesson 87's title came to mind: 'I will there be light.' In retrospect, who doesn't want only the light in their lives?

It's our inherent right, from the second we're born. But we're afraid of the unseen and intangible, as the lesson notes. We want to go with our heart, to be free, but it's so difficult.

Avraham decided that the second half of the meeting would be an opportunity for group members to express their thoughts about the first half.

Manu shifted with discomfort, his chin on his chest. "I can't talk right now. I'm sorry. But I would like permission to talk at the next meeting."

Eva studied him. He was, without a doubt, a man who made an impression: handsome, financially successful. From coffee-corner chats she knew he was happily married to a successful woman, they had four children who he loved with all his heart, that he couldn't live without them, and that he owes a good deal of his success to his wife who was there for him, supporting and assisting, urging him forward while simultaneously advancing her own career. Why he was in the course was a puzzle to Eva, but she'd learned that appearances don't attest to a person's inner being.

"I just want to hug you both, Emily and Eva, and infuse you both with strength," said Nathan, who had shared his own story the previous week and now sat with tears in his eyes.

In silence, Eva and Emily quickly glanced at each other.

"I have nothing to say at the moment," Sarai said.

"Me neither," Odette piped up. "The words are stuck in my throat." The others nodded in agreement.

There'll probably be more bombs going off from those who've yet to do their reveals, Eva thought.

"I think we've been shaken up," Avraham said, "and we have plenty to read and think about over the coming week. Mostly, I want you to think about how you forgive yourselves and people who've hurt you. Instead of thinking we're life's victims, can we think about the idea of how we are the reflection of our lives? Maybe if we look in the mirror and talk to the image we see, we can forgive," he said.

"Forgiving doesn't mean accepting the matter as it is. It means looking at what's happened, even if it's the worst thing imaginable, with open eyes and accepting the bad as well as the good, and especially not allowing the bad to manage how we continue to handle things. We need to try and thank the Shekhinah for bringing even difficult situations into our lives. If we do, that allows good energy to seep inside us. The fact that you've come to the course and decided not to live in silence anymore, but to reveal the less pleasant parts of your lives, is the start of recovery.

"If we don't talk about the good or the bad with anyone, then they lose their value. If they're bottled up inside, they just bring us to anger. Similarly, if we don't talk about the good, who'll know about it? Who'll pat us on the back? Everyone needs that—top level managers, highly successful people: without that bit of acknowledgment there's no significance to what we're doing.

"From experience I can say that, even the most humble person, the one who gives to others without it being known, also needs a kind word on occasion. We determine our framework of integrity, for good or bad, and that framework sets the degree of our exposure to being hurt. When we lack vitality, are vulnerable, or not appreciated, our entire functioning diminishes. That's when our bodies send out warning signals that they can't cope, and we start getting sick.

"When you're back home," he added, "drink some cool water, listen to some music that you love, try to think of the essence of today's class, and only start working at the book again from tomorrow on."

In their concern for her, some had already been remarking to Eva that she wasn't looking great. She could feel it: her body was on the verge of collapse. She'd lost a lot of weight because she could hardly swallow, even though medically, nothing was wrong with her throat despite the lump that was always present. She knew that day in and day out, over time these conditions could bring on physical symptoms and illnesses. At some point she told herself that she really hadn't done anything bad to anyone. She wanted to continue living a happy, meaningful life enjoying her children, her grandchildren and those yet to come. With every passing day she realized that if a change inside herself didn't happen soon, it could be too late.

Nonetheless, the images, memories and emotions kept surfacing in her mind, squawking like fledglings pecking at wood and, despite seeming menial each on their own, their constant activity grew strong, powerful, repetitive, allowing her no rest. Eva returned home so flooded that she couldn't sleep. Even her glass of sherry didn't help.

She turned on Swan Lake: music of passion, love, beauty, and tragedy. Perhaps not exactly what Avraham had in mind with his suggestion, but the music brought back the images of the ballet she'd attended in New York and again in London, performed by top ranking international dance troupes. Little by little, the music calmed her.

She was being battered by a storm: the deception and insult that had occurred just before she arrived at the session, the fact that her husband had once again breached the terms of their trial separation. She was not willing to meet him that evening. She didn't answer his calls or texts. What value could there be in talking to him? It was clear: there was no way back. Clearly, divorce was next. That thought choked her.

By contrast, her compassion for Emily's situation completely confused her. Feeling that way was forbidden. Taboo. How could she possibly empathize with Emily, a woman who was knowingly continuing an affair with a married, family man.

She was having trouble squaring the oppositional thoughts. But there's no doubt, she reasoned, that my compassion could only come as a result of what I'm learning in the course. Every class was guiding us towards forgiveness, especially towards ourselves; guiding us to seeing the other in a different light, the light of Shekhinah, even if that other has hurt us. I need to understand that without forgiveness I'll continue wearing blinders; as Lesson 247 states: "Without forgiveness I will still be blind." Still, Eva wasn't sure she was emotionally ready for that.

Psychologically exhausted, the next morning she couldn't drag herself out of bed. Luckily, she had no meetings set up, only work from home. Deciding that taking the morning slowly would be perfectly alright, she let herself be distracted by a random TV show. Only towards early afternoon did she open the computer. The thoughts were still rolling around but less disruptively. Perhaps now she could make some leeway.

She texted her husband. "Nothing to discuss at this point. No stories or excuses are acceptable. I request no contact for the coming week."

He didn't even answer.

The unpleasantness relating to Emily resurfaced. She remembered how she'd felt at the suggestion of splitting her home and renting rooms to for extra income. She almost slapped the person raising the idea. "Why should I go along with that?" she'd screamed at the time. Now she was feeling a thread connecting her with Emily. It scared her. It bamboozled her.

But her decision to halt contact with her husband made her feel that she was taking charge of her life again. Just by virtue of not talking to him and not hearing his volley of excuses made her feel she was regaining control over her life's reins. That, along with the complexity around Emily, kept her mind busy all week.

On one hand, "I'm regaining control," but on the other, "I do not have the courage and psychological energy."

CHAPTER 10

"There is nothing to fear."

The next meeting would take place three weeks before the festival of Passover. Eva was bombarded by emotions. She was fond of Emily, yet had difficulty accepting Emily's choices. Eva knew she had no right to judge, but it was still a challenging task. Throughout the course we keep learning that we're all one, Eva reminded herself. We come into the same world within the framework of the Shekhinah. We get to choose and decide, yet perhaps I need to look at Emily from a different perspective, Eva reasoned. If I can do that relative to Emily, can I do it also relative to the 'other woman' in my story?

"So how do we forgive?" she had asked Avraham.

But he wasn't giving away easy formulas. "You'll know that when you're ready," he said, gazing tranquilly into her eyes.

She knew she didn't know, hadn't yet arrived at that stage. She was in a stormy sea. The waves were massive. They tossed her up and plummeted her down. She struggled. Sometimes she floated. Sometimes she found herself on a crest, able to look around, catch her breath. Then the trough would come and she'd be out of air, suffocating, anxiety taking over. What was she anxious about? She couldn't define it. She tried reaching its source in her therapy sessions.

Her son's and daughter-in-law's wedding anniversary came

around. She was excited about that, but alongside were so many other emotions.

What would happen if she divorced? Could she see herself that way? Would it harm her family? After all, it's a type of failure, she told herself. Her second time on the Rabbinate's steps to register a change of family status, and certainly not to dance happily at a wedding. She remembered the first marriage: they'd both been so young, rash, and it had barely lasted eighteen months, impacted all the more because of a war. But this second marriage was meant to last forever.

She couldn't stop torturing herself with two questions: where did she go wrong, and how didn't she see this coming?

Repeatedly, her therapist reassured her she wasn't to blame for the failure, and that it would have happened one way or another. Then Eva was whelmed by fear of being alone: she was someone who felt most comfortable as part of a couple. She loved to share. To do things together. To give. That never meant voiding her independence; on the contrary: being part of a couple gave her confidence. Even having to choose a wedding dress without others coming with her to interfere with her decision was a difficult moment.

Then a new fear surfaced: her age. Everyone wants them young, Standing in front of the mirror, Eva summed herself up, physically. Her breasts were no longer pert, wrinkles were starting to show on her face, her body was no longer firmly shaped the way it used to be. Who'd want her? She suddenly realized: the right person would want her just as she is. And with that thought she slipped into bed and fell asleep.

As her capabilities, which she'd repressed for so long, in alternative communication, understanding things that were in the realm of the supposedly supranatural or that which is beyond nature, sharpened over the years, she realized just how much her husband had mocked her and how little of that part of her she'd shared with him. But when her life blew up, these sensitivities and the knowledge that came from it became stronger and empowered her. She often communicated with her grandfather at night. That infused her with strength. She communicated with a childhood friend who died young: the friend kept reassuring her she had no reason to worry. The friend took on the visage of a beautiful, radiant child with blond hair and a string of pearls around her neck, and told her she'd always be there for Eva: all she had to do was reach out for the pearls.

A few days ago she'd woken with the sudden realization that she urgently needed to check the signatures on their bank accounts. On many occasions over the past two years Eva had woken with a snippet of information which never disappointed and, in most cases, upset her world. She asked her husband to set up a meeting at the bank. Sitting there facing a clerk who was not the same one her husband usually met with, the light bulb went off: nothing is coincidental. Eva asked to see the signatures on all accounts. Everything was in order, until the clerk suddenly looked up.

"Wait a sec," she said. "There's an account here with three signatures. Why?"

Eva's husband tried to hush the matter up, then wave it away, then mumble something about possible errors.

"Your wife wishes to see all your accounts and this one has three signatories," the clerk repeated, taking out the document. Immediately Eva identified the third name and signature: her husband's lover. Eva almost fainted. The clerk brought her a glass of water and waited for her to regain her composure. Her husband was busy explaining that the signatory was the company's accountant who was preparing materials for the CPA. Eva was shocked into silence.

But not for long. She demanded from the equally surprised clerk and the bank manager, who she asked the clerk to call over, to have the signature cancelled on the spot. Eva and her husband walked to the car, Eva's eyes burning with fury, her heart racing. She should never have presumed she didn't need to check their banking affairs. One thing was clear: knowing what was happening in the account, and how to control the accounts, was power. No woman, no matter how good the relationship with her partner, should waive her right to know these details at all times.

Right then, as wave after wave crashed inside her, she found it hard to believe that good things were still in store for her. That's when she'd think of her parents' marriage, of the terrible events they experienced in the Holocaust, how they'd risen above it all to establish a family and continued to live as happily as they could, loving each other and having compassion for almost everyone. That morning she decided to inform her parents of her life's turn. There was no point in hiding it anymore.

She plucked up her courage and went to her parents' home. They always greeted her with smiles, but her mother saw right away that something major was brewing.

"One of the boys in the army?" her mother asked.

"No, no, thank goodness not that. They're alright, don't worry." Eva sighed. "But I do have some, ah, news... " she said, gesturing to the living room. The three of them sat down.

"I'm getting divorced," Eva said softly. Her parents sat in a stunned silence before asking if either of them had someone else in the picture.

"It's mostly," Eva evaded answering directly, "because the kids are grown up and we're in a crisis we can't resolve, even with couples counseling."

Her parents' eyes were piercing. "You're clearly hiding something," they said almost simultaneously. Eva broke, and told them the details. It shattered them emotionally. They began to vent their anger and derision for the man they had loved so much.

"We'll help you, no matter what you need," they added right away, hugging her as they cried.

The idea that she, a grandmother herself, needed their emotional support was tough to take. Little wonder it took her two years to get up the courage and tell them. But she also felt tremendous relief, as though having removed a heavy burden from her shoulders. Things would be easier now that she didn't need to hide the situation from her parents.

By the time Eva joined the meeting everyone else had already arrived. Avraham asked them to draw closer into the circle and link hands. Even though not everyone had yet shared their stories, they all felt a very strong bond. The group promoted connectivity and gratitude for attentive listening and support. They spoke of containment, of being able to give vent to their deepest emotions without being judged, of the warm embrace that gave them a foundation and strength. Eva thought it sounded just like a close friend, the kind who can hug you when you're low, as she was lately, when everything that was niggling at her over the years but couldn't quite explain came to a head.

She remembered how great it had felt to get together with her friend, Gaia, and how much Dita had helped with kind words, her bottle of sherry, and listening without inserting advice.

Right before Avraham began the meditation session Eva smiled quickly at Emily, who smiled back in appreciation with a nod of her head.

The meeting began with Lesson 48: 'There is nothing to fear.' For all intents and purposes, a simple concept, but so difficult for someone who prefers to exist out of touch with reality. Manu, who from the group's start had been propping his head up, rubbed his hands together and asked to speak.

"I feel that my whole life is one huge illusion and I don't really have a clue how I can get to a point where my greatest weakness can be my strength."

He glanced at Emily, then at Eva, then bowed his head,

talking quietly as though to himself, as is he was afraid he might say something that would perhaps hurt someone.

"Since the previous meeting where Emily told us her story and in light of the difficulty I hear from you, Eva, across all the meetings so far, I want to apologize from the depths of my heart to you, to my wife, and to my children too, because if I thought I was hiding everything, then I'm not such a smart guy at all."

That got the group's attention and they all turned to look at him, waiting for what he could possibly have to say. Why the apology? His height, the clothes that sat well on his toned body, and the snippets of silver hair at his temples gave him a strong presence. He was a successful businessman, owned several companies, traveled back and forth being away for the better part of each year, employed hundreds of people, was an inventor who operated in the realm of security, but now sat cringing in his chair, unable to make eye contact with any of them.

"I'm the married man," he paused, "who's been in a long-term affair with a married woman." He paused again. "And she's not the first, even though my wife is amazing, gorgeous, talented, successful, and a wonderful mother to our two children. Yet I'm unable to remain faithful to her. The main reason I joined the course is that my therapist recommended it and because, even after I became aware, through therapy, that I'm behaving the way my father did to my mother, I still couldn't break off the current affair, which is also the longest I've ever had.

"I don't know if my wife knows, but I presume she senses something's up with me. I always sleep at home, but I also travel a ton and the 'other woman' joins me at those locations. It's clear to me now, as it is to all of you, that ongoing extramarital relationships can't be hidden for years.

"I'm in complete disarray since the last few meetings. I truly understand, from the depths of my heart, how much I'm hurting my wife and children, as well as the other woman who likely expects that one day I'll leave my wife and home for her, but I'm unwilling to take that step. It's terribly selfish. I can't explain, even to myself, why I'm do this. Perhaps it's a drive, an addiction to a conquer more and more?

"But now, from what you've said, I understand how deep the betrayal is and what damage it causes. I hear you, Eva, talking about the lump in your throat that you can actually feel even though tests show nothing's actually there. I live with chronic pain for a while now: terrible back pain. My doctor's constantly asking if something's going on in my life because there's no medical reason for it.

"The crunch came for me when my young son finished high school. It was such a milestone. He's an excellent student, highly admired. He participated in the graduation show by performing a dance with a female classmate, which is the kind of thing he would never normally do. And instead of sitting there in the audience with my wife, with my other children, with my wife's parents, praising him for moving out of his comfort zone and successfully too, where was I? Off on a business trip that could have easily been postponed. Of course, with the woman I'm having an affair with. My son is on stage performing, my wife is sending me videos so I can see it all live, and there I am in a hotel room in a different country with my mistress. And I just can't fathom why I behave that way."

He stopped for a moment, as though the weight of what he was saying was almost too heavy to bear. "I'm not seeking your support, nor even a drop of understanding. On the contrary: I'm asking you to compel me to agonize over questions, even when you hear the story's end. I want to hear what you have to say, especially because I promised myself repeatedly to never have an affair again but I've never kept that promise."

"My mother and I always meet once a week, just the two of us. We've been doing that since my father passed away. The day after our meeting last week, I got up the guts and asked, for the first time ever, if she knew about my father's transgressions. Tears flooded her eyes.

"She answered softly. 'Yes, but see, that was a different generation. We didn't talk about such private matters then, we didn't go to therapy, there weren't any empowerment workshops. I couldn't share with my friends, not even the closest, about what I was going through. Your father repeatedly promised it would stop, he'd say there's no meaning to these relationships, that he loves me and only me, and that they're not romances based on love, just kind of a show of manhood. That was normal in his environment of successful industrialists. He said that sometimes he didn't even know the names of the women. That was supposed to pacify me.'

"The tears began streaming down her face. I put her hand in mind and said that I'm so sorry. She didn't understand why I was apologizing, so I told her everything. She whisked her hand out of mine and gave me a resounding slap on the cheek. Nothing has ever hurt me more than that slap. On the other hand, I have never received a more deserving slap.

"Luckily for me we were seated at the furthest part of the restaurant in a more or less private booth, but that slap rang so loud that the waitress came over fast to ask if everything was okay. My mother smiled warmly. I grinned sheepishly. That slap wasn't meant just for me, I knew it was also meant for my father. It was the one she never had the courage to give him.

"And then she hugged me. Gazing at me intently, she spoke. 'I hope that slap echoes in your heart for years to come. I hope you not only feel the physical pain, but the emotional pain you have caused, first of all to your wife, then to your children, then to this other woman who you're deceiving for your own selfish needs.' Her eyes sparked with flashes of fury."

The group sat riveted to their chairs. Eva's mouth was agape. Tears poured from Emily's eyes. The others gazed at Manu, at Emily, at Eva and lastly, at Avraham.

"May I get a glass of water?" Manu asked quietly.

"Of course. Let's take a break," Avraham answered.

Eva could feel the nausea climbing up to her throat, as though her body wanted to cleanse itself from Manu's story, which was clearly her story too. Indeed, she felt no compassion for him, nor did she wish to. That slap his mother landed spoke for her as well, and for all the betrayed men and women, husbands and wives whose significant other was involved in an affair. Yes, obviously there were two sides to the coin but, as she began to learn about the women who were entangled in these affairs, it always turned out that they suffered from an extreme lack of emotional empathy at home and from their partners.

It hardly ever had to do with sex, per se, or the need to prove that they were still sexually viable or attractive, even when older. Nor did these women enter affairs with married men for the sake of feeling supremacy or power, as so many men did. For many women, a vibrator solved the sexual issue without the need to complicate it with a web of lies, deceit and clandestine adventures.

Without a doubt, the women were more practical: for career-minded women, every absence from their homes, the family and their children caused them to feel guilt, far more than men felt for doing the same. She smiled, remembering countless work meetings where she was the only woman present. The men often lapsed into stories of their military service or some business success. Just as often she'd need to move things along. "Guys," she'd say, "my wife isn't waiting at home to pick up the kids." They'd laugh, get the message, and get back to the work discussion.

And still, the question hammered in her brain: If things aren't good, why not talk about it? Why cheat? Why cause such long-term pain? She tried understanding the dynamic relative to her husband, but couldn't come up with a satisfactory answer.

After the coffee break, fairly subdued this time, the group reconvened and Manu continued.

"After talking to my mother last week, I was truly afraid of your reaction," he gave a sad grin. "Two days ago I met with 'the other woman,' as you call her, Eva, and told her that I'm ending the relationship. I asked her forgiveness for giving her any hope that perhaps one day I'd leave my home, but due to going to therapy and this course, I realized I'd never leave my wife, my home, and my children.

"She turned white. When she recovered enough to speak, she said that she'd reached that conclusion a long time ago, and that she did love her husband and didn't want to cause him and his family any pain, but couldn't get herself to break from me. She kissed my cheek, thanked me for everything, promised to keep our good memories in her heart forever and also promised to erase my name and details from her phone. We also agreed that should we bump into each other at some social event, since we have many of those circles in common, we'd just nod in acknowledgment and nothing more. I was stunned that she didn't ask to make love one last time. I guess that was my fantasy. And so it ended, our years-long romance.

"Then an amazing thing happened: my back stopped aching. I went home earlier than usual, told my wife that the meeting had been canceled at the last second, and promised myself never to lie to her again. Last night we sat down together for dinner. I didn't even bring my phone to the table, confident that no sudden messages or calls would come through and, if they did, I wouldn't have to hide them from her.

"I was so relaxed, which surprised me, and my wife and I even raised the idea of a romantic vacation. We decided to look for destinations after dinner. The kids came up and hugged me. I've no idea why. I also have no idea how this magical moment came into being. I had a sense that my wife had picked up on something. Maybe it was my imagination, but I saw a smile flit across her face that seemed to say, 'Everything's fine, I know about it all, and now we can turn over a new leaf, enjoying the rest our lives together.' That night our bed felt so comfortable. I looked around at the elegant bedroom which my wife always lovingly maintained. A duo of fresh-cut roses stood in a tall slim vase on my nightstand. How had I never seen all these details before?

"It was an amazing night, one of the most passionate I can remember. The atmosphere was charged with a feeling of relief, an absence of the constant tension I had been wrangling with for so many years. I won't go into details, but my wife's scent was so wonderful that... her semi-transparent white nightgown which she'd worn many times before was suddenly so sexy to me. Her body was a charm. I was discovering a sensuality in her that I don't think I'd ever experienced with any of my lovers.

"The next morning I awoke with a huge smile. The night before, we had decided that we'd have a day off, just for us. She was still asleep, and I couldn't stop gazing at how beautiful she was. I remembered how and when I'd fallen in love with her. I closed my eyes, horrified: how could I have hurt her so deeply!?"

Manu halted, as though replaying the scene in his mind. "That's when it clicked, the meaning of the words 'unconditional love.' I kept reading the texts about forgiveness, meaningfulness and love, over and over. All day I was looking forward to this meeting so that I could tell you the whole story. I knew it would also be painful for some to hear, but hoped that perhaps it would also bring a message of love and acceptance. Despite the difficulty involved, I'm fully prepared to answer even your toughest questions, and ask for your forgiveness, which is so important to me."

Missed opportunity, Eva thought. And envy, because she realized her husband would never come back to her. From the moment that the infidelities, and the awareness of which she'd try to suppress over the years, became a fact, she wouldn't be able to save the relationship, even if her children's father wanted to pursue that course of action. She only hoped that, over time, he'd have the courage to apologize without adding 'but' and immediately offering an excuse by way of justification.

Deep inside, though, she knew that waiting for an apology was pointless. It would never happen, because her husband would never admit that he was at fault. She longed for the day when she no longer had any interest in his apology. She'd come a long way and it had been grueling, changing her way of life, deciding that the pain wasn't worth the time it devoured, and that she needed to free up space for her present and future. The goal was for the forgiveness to come from within herself and free her heart.

Conversely, Emily was extremely embarrassed.

"I need to take the next step but I don't know how," she said shortly before the meeting's end. "In my case, it's not just about ending a forbidden relationship, but there's also a financial aspect. First I have to find alternative employment. So, as a first step," her voice firmed up, "I've decided now, sitting here with you all, to tell my lover who is also my boss that I'm down with flu. He won't visit me to help, anyhow."

She gave a wonky smile and stood as the rest of the group watched, taken by surprise. "Can I talk to you later this week?" she asked Eva.

"Of course," Eva agreed immediately.

The meeting ended. Despite how difficult it felt to do, Eva hugged Manu and thanked him.

Thinking about Nathan's story, as well as Emily's and Odette's, she realized that each of them could have made their lives easier had they shared the secret with someone rather than keeping it locked up inside, feeling ashamed. Clearly shame must be a forceful emotion; to talk about a situation that you're embarrassed to be in, that belittles yourself, is tough. You want support but are fearful of criticism. The most inspiring and scary moment is the one when you realize there's no shame in falling.

In the car, contradicting thoughts collided and swirled. She so badly wanted to have someone else to talk to, to expand her circle of friends whom she admittingly neglected over the years, to share how her life had panned out, and not only in the course or with her therapist. She decided to call two childhood friends with whom she'd lost contact even though they lived fairly close by. How would they respond to her sudden reconnection? Very well, apparently, as they immediately arranged to meet at a café for breakfast, which stretched into lunch and well into the afternoon. The waiter was baffled at how three adult women could spend so many hours talking, crying, laughing, hugging.

Eva told them everything. They were stunned. Eva had no idea what they've been through, their ups and downs. They were sorry they hadn't stayed in touch through all these life events and promised to be there for one another, help each other out, listen and, most importantly, be nonjudgmental and supportive.

Back home that evening Eva was floating in a cloud of relief. Emily came to mind. The complex situation with Manu came to mind. Over and over her feelings towards Emily oscillated between compassion and anger.

The next morning Emily phoned, crying and barely able to talk between the all the gulps for air.

"I have to break it off," she sobbed. "I now know that I deserve a fuller, better life than this. I'm worth more than being hidden away in the closet like a guilty secret."

Eva listened closely. "Do you want me to go and talk to your boss?" she suddenly found herself offering.

"You don't know how happy I am to hear you say that. What a relief. I was hoping that would be your reaction, but I wasn't brave enough to ask for it outright. Thank you, Eva. I'll try to get some sense of whether he's open to such a conversation."

An hour later a message came through on Eva's phone. "Yes, he's willing!" with a smiley.

Not wanting to lose momentum, the women agreed that Eva would go to Emily's place of work the next morning. Eva didn't know why she was pushing herself into this. However, she did truly want to help Emily, and perhaps also help the boss's wife and family. Perhaps deep inside she was doing what she'd hoped someone would have done for her.

Eva arrived. It was an industrial zone, lacking any charm, attractive colors or pleasant atmosphere. How did Emily find employment in this of all places? But it explained much of what Emily hadn't put into words.

"Give us a couple of minutes?" Eva said to Emily once in the office. Emily, still amazed that Eva showed up and took on the role, nodded and left the room.

Eva, her back straight, her gaze direct and piercing, sat down facing Emily's boss.

"I am the legal wife," Eva said, her voice firm. "I am the one who was cheated on for years. I want to tell you about the pain, the insult, the humiliation, the helplessness, the insecurity and breathlessness it causes, for days and nights on end."

Without giving him time to say a word, Eva told Emily's boss about the physical and emotional pain, the sleepless nights, the agony that seared every cell in her body, the fears, the vain attempts to cover it all up for the children's sakes, even though they were now adults. She described him about the shame and embarrassment, even though she had no reason to be ashamed. Sitting facing him, she shot arrow after arrow.

He sat behind his large, impressive desk, shocked. A tear welled in his eyes. This businessman, with his deep bass voice, in charge of countless employees, and apparently in control of his wife and children too, seemed to shrink from minute to minute in his high-backed luxury manager's chair. Upholstered in light mocha top-grade leather, it was a comfortable chair for rocking in while pondering. But the boss didn't move, didn't smile. He sat silently and stoically, listening.

Eva halted, steeled herself, and asked point blank. "Do you love Emily enough to leave your wife and children?"

"I won't leave my wife," he answered without hesitation.

Eva stayed silent. She could feel Emily's pain on hearing her boss's statement.

"If I call Emily in, will you tell her exactly what you said to me?"

Emily's boss began to rock on his chair, as nervous as a child who knows that his favorite toy is about to be taken from him. But he quickly composed himself.

"Yes," he eventually said.

Holding the door open behind her, Eva called Emily, who reentered the office without any idea of what had transpired. In truth, Eva hadn't planned any specific strategy either. She simply let things flow. Eva remembered Avraham's words: "You were meant to be in my place." For a flash it seemed as if she understood what he meant. Emily's smile quickly changed to a look of worry when she turned to Eva and her boss/lover.

"The moment of truth has arrived," Eva said after Emily sat down. "Tell Emily what you told me just a moment ago." The powerful businessman squirmed in his seat, cleared his throat a couple of times and eventually, in a whisper, without his charismatic and authority-laden bass, spoke:

"Emily, I love you, but I'll never leave my wife and family."

Emily didn't notice Eva taking her hand: the cheated woman and the cheating woman sat together, joined in a moment of comprehension that shocked Eva. She was as uneasy as when she'd first heard Emily's story. Her hands were sweating, but Emily didn't let go. They stood, still hand in hand. Emily was squeezing Eva's hand tightly; Eva kept her grip firm. Emily's boss did not stand or accompany them out. He remained glued in his seat.

Emily drew Eva to her part of the office to collect her personal items. Eva assisted. Neither woman looked at the boss. They went downstairs, leaving the gallery level from which the boss could view the entire factory. They knew he was watching, but ignored him and walked on. Emily suddenly looked up. In an instant she realized that the employees, all of them, knew about her affair. She held her head up, trying to keep her emotions in check.

"Did you bring your car?" Eva asked Emily.

"No. It wouldn't start this morning so I took a taxi." They smiled. Emily's car, of course, was simply reflecting her state of mind.

"C'mon, I'll take you home."

"Now we both need to live the rest of our lives as well as we can," Emily said once they were both seated in Eva's car. "Without fear. We're strong women." Eva agreed. They hugged each other.

At the next meeting, Eva kept a place next to her for Emily. Manu and Odette sat next to them. An atmosphere of comradeship common to those who've been through an emotional upheaval together linked them. Eva was sure this was the start of a long-lasting friendship.

CHAPTER 11

"I am not alone in experiencing the effects of my seeing."

Walking into the room, Avraham smiled at everyone, watching them intently as he always did. He gazed into Eva's eyes and smiled, nodding his head towards her. She noticed that he didn't seem comfortable in his chair and, despite the warm weather, had a heavy scarf wrapped around his neck.

The class began with 'I see no neutral things,' 'I am not alone in experiencing the effects of my seeing,' and 'I am determined to see.' When Avraham read, "I have no neutral thoughts," Rachel burst into tears of desperation and a cry for help.

Eva was sure she knew Rachel from somewhere. Rachel felt the same way. No matter how much they raised ideas for possible common points of contact, they found none. They were already laughing at the idea that perhaps they knew each other from a previous life. Avraham repeating that nothing was coincidental only underlined the oddity in the fact that they'd both decided on the same day to join the same course.

"We're all linked to each other," he would often remind them, "even if we're sure there's no connection. Slowly what envelopes us unravels and we see the connections surfacing by virtue of being together in this group."

After calming down a little, Rachel asked if she could tell her story.

"Something in the last chapter I read is hard for me to contain and floods me with emotions I can't handle, especially in light of the statement that we're all children of God and the Shekhinah was given to us all to bring goodness, and that we're all one energy."

Rachel dabbed at her nose. "So why is there such terrible vulnerability? I understand that everything we go through in life is part of the divine framework and, despite the difficulty, I understand that we're the ones who bring parts of our journey into our own lives. But I have difficulty accepting these notions, and I'll try to explain why I'm so upset.

"I'm attempting to get a grip on the idea that, in the end, we who choose how to cope, and we seek out what will give us peace, or the change that's needed, even if we didn't think we were looking for it."

Rachel paused to take a few breaths before continuing. "I didn't know how comfortable and convenient routine could be. It's not the perfect way of being but it's known, it's familiar. And then something comes along and completely shakes us up, and every shakeup demands that we jump into the deep end where the water can be murky, or frozen."

Rachel is a beautiful, tall woman with curly Titian hair, elegantly dressed, always wearing modest outfits, and only later Eva would understand what she hid behind her clothes, which were sometimes buttoned all the way up to her neck.

"A year ago my fourteen year old daughter came raging into our home, which is in a gated community with a guard on duty. We're on the twentieth floor with a stunning three-sixty view of Tel Aviv. She was shaking, crying hysterically. I was on the verge of slapping her hard just to shake her out of what seemed to be shock. She told me that a man was standing right in front of the building. He was around her grandfather's age, looked like a businessman, dressed in a suit and a tie, with a large pot belly. One of the types of people commonly seen in the neighborhood.

"And then she says this: 'The man came over to me and started asking me a question. He mumbled and I couldn't hear what he was saying. Suddenly he grabbed my hand and pushed me violently towards the corner that's hidden by the rubber tree. I started screaming,' she was sobbing hard, 'but the man wouldn't let go. Another man passed and looked. Maybe he thought we were a father and daughter arguing and just walked on while I'm screaming for my life.

'Luckily, the lobby guard thought he heard something was amiss and came out. One glance and he figured what was happening. He ran towards the man with his gun aimed it at him. The man let go of me, the guard shouted at me to get home fast, and chased the man. I saw neighbors coming to help the guard. They took the suited man down to the ground and got their phones out, probably to call the police, and I raced home.' I hugged my daughter, wanting to calm her, and she begins vomiting. Repeatedly. A flash from my own childhood came into my mind and next thing I was doubled over too, also vomiting.

"My husband walked in just then and sees the two women he loves in a terrible state, both of us weeping, collapsing on each other. It took him a long time to get us both cleaned up and calmed down, which we managed to do only because we knew we were in safe hands. I started telling him what our daughter had described and how she'd been saved. He'd seen the man being pushed into a police van. He knew it would take us time to overcome the trauma and, right away, he canceled his business trip abroad scheduled for two days from then.

"Meanwhile the police contacted us and asked that we come to the youth services detective's offices to give testimony. My husband asked if we could postpone that until the next day to give our daughter time to recover.

"And as my daughter stood there crying, shaking, because of the pot-bellied attacker, it came to me. My uncle. My father's brother. The successful businessman with the pot belly. Always in suits and ties, his hair always in place, always with some expensive gift for his 'favorite niece.' He harassed and abused me sexually for an entire year when I was ten. I don't remember why it stopped. Maybe someone in the family picked up on something.

"At that time, I began to do poorly in school; I became withdrawn. I used to be surrounded by friends but during and after that year I didn't want to leave the house or go anywhere anymore, not even to my grandparents who I'd always loved visiting but is where the nightmare of my life took place. So when my daughter told me what happened, everything she said connected to my experiences and made me vomit my own pain out too.

"My daughter, clutching a large stuffed bear, fell asleep in my arms after I gave her some Bach Rescue drops. I sat down with my husband and told him of the memories that had flooded me. He was so understanding. 'Now we know why you have such a visceral reaction when you see men who look like that,' he said gently. He remembered the boss I worked for before my marriage, a good man with infectious joie de vivre who made sure the atmosphere in the office was always pleasant, had good relations with the staff, and was very knowledgeable. We spoke about how he appreciated my marketing abilities and kept promoting me, but I couldn't stand being in his presence. He was, let's say, heavy set, with a huge belly. As we spoke, suddenly things clicked into place. It even made me smile.

"So many insights surfaced in one fell swoop. That uncle died some years earlier. I couldn't understand why suddenly my temperature went up so high that I couldn't go to the funeral or make the standard visit to the home where the mourners gathered. Clearly my subconscious was protecting me. Year after year, on the date of his annual memorial, I came down with a sore throat and high temperature.

"One night, a week after my daughter's attack, I called the sexual abuse hotline and told my story to a woman who listened and listened with endless patience."

In a flash of a glance, Rachel and Eva realized how they knew each other. They didn't know each other by face, only voice. Eva had received that call on her volunteer night shift.

"Between my sobs, between my silences, she gave me the strength to share what happened to me with my family, to tell them about my childhood. She suggested a psychologist to work with my daughter and, separately, with me. She also praised my husband for his amazing support for our daughter and me.

Rachel look around, a faint smile playing on her lips. "You all know that Eva and I keep trying to figure out how we know each other. A second ago, we discovered it. She was the voice on the hotline that night. She was the one who gave me so much hope. She put me in touch with a wonderful psychologist who recommended this course."

"My daughter also started therapy. Initially she wasn't willing to leave home on her own, so we drove her everywhere. Slowly she began agreeing that, if we went down in the elevator with her and a friend was waiting downstairs, she'd go with the friend. Her phone was always fully charged, and she asked us to put a tracking app on her phone so we'd know where she was at all times.

"But deep inside I know that it'll take years for her to be free of the trauma. We, her family, will always be there for her and maybe knowing that will also help her get through it."

Rachel smiled at Eva. "I guess you must have said your name when I phoned but I didn't remember it. I used a pseudonym. But after two conversations with Eva, I worked up the courage to talk to my parents and grandparents. Amazingly, my grandparents weren't surprised. It turns out that they knew about their highly successful son's tendencies toward sexual violence but never had the guts to tell any of their other children, even when they feared that I wasn't the only one he preyed on but was abusive to other girls in the extended family as well.

"My father and his siblings reacted very harshly to this news. Those were days of complete shock, of torrents of anger cast at each other, especially my father and his siblings against their parents. Our sense of family unity came apart at the seams.

My uncle moved at a relatively young age to Australia, as far from the family as possible. He cut all contact with them. Nor did he attend his father's funeral. Perhaps his parents demanded that he keep his distance, but we'll never know that now. My grandfather passed away this year, after my daughter was attacked, and my grandmother developed Alzheimer's which deteriorated at an accelerated rate, surprising not only the family but her doctors.

"A year after difficult, awkward silences we began meeting again as a family but things were never the same. The talented, successful uncle ripped the family's foundations to shreds. Perhaps with the help of this course and my psychologist, I'll be able to bring everyone together and somehow get us to keep moving forward, and put the shame to the family's honor aside. Today, it's clear to me that sexual abuse occurs across all sectors of the population, whatever the social, educational or economic status. So many of us carry these terrible secrets. They are the proverbial massive elephant in the middle of every family event.

"Avraham," Rachel turned to look at him, "I hope that I can find some healing for my soul, understand why it happened and how to forgive, not so much the act, but the power it wielded, because I'd like to know what the goal is, what type of purpose that uncle fills in our lives, even if such knowledge is difficult to contain. Maybe this year-long course will help me heal the rift among my family members, who are still very dear to me.

"I have trouble digesting what I experienced. I'm extremely angry at the experience my daughter went through. Had she not been attacked, I might never have been triggered into remembering my own childhood. I wouldn't have gotten into a conflict with my grandparents. All the love I'd had for them simply evaporated. But it's hard to understand why they hid those facts about my uncle from everyone, or how they allowed him be around us, their granddaughters, who they supposedly love so much.

"Precisely in the place where we should have felt safe, where our parents sent us feeling confident that we were being well looked after, everything exploded. Unwittingly, they sent us into the lion's den. They didn't have a clue, our parents. But our grandparents did. They could have insisted he stay away when we were there. How could they have done that to us?"

Rachel raged at the world, but turned to Avraham as the group leader. "How can anyone understand or accept or contain something like that? I'm telling you about what happened to my body and I feel as though my grandparents also desecrated it through their progeny, their son. I'm trying to understand how people can do such things. I wonder: if I could discover more about their childhoods in Germany, I might be able to understand the background to the destructiveness. It wouldn't justify what they did to me but perhaps I could find a way to forgive. Is that even possible?"

Rachel took a deep breath and shook her head slowly. "Okay. So now I want to ask a tough question. Do I need to accept that my daughter underwent what she did so that our entire family could be rattled into wakefulness? And if so, why rouse these things up? How can I find answers? Sometimes I wonder if it's not better, as they say, to let sleeping dogs lie. Anyhow we won't find out much from the others. My grandfather took his secrets from Germany to the grave. He simply muttered an apology before he closed his eyes forever. My grandmother has moments of lucidity and sometimes I wonder if they're meant for us, meant to give us time for those questions."

Avraham, who suddenly looked wan, gazed directly into Rachel's eyes.

"What do you really want? Would you want her to spend those clear-eyed moments answering you? And answering which question exactly?"

Rachel sat hunched, clasping and unclasping her hands, squirming on her seat. She gripped the chair's arms suddenly as though hanging on for dear life, as though if she were to let go her life would collapse.

"I know I won't crumple. I know what spiritual and emotional powers I found inside myself. This crisis has brought my husband and me closer. We began looking at each other much more sympathetically, more lovingly. Could that be why all this happened? I.. don't know."

Her hands were back on the chair's arms. "My husband began to be more present at home, be more available to our only daughter and to me. I pushed him quite hard to go to therapy too, because he was furious at my grandparents, and justifiably. How couldn't one be furious?"

Rachel paused, gazing intently at Avraham. When she spoke, she sounded as though she was wondering out loud. "Some of my cousins were very young when my uncle left. I hope it was to their advantage. But I sense that more of these situations will come to light and blow up in our faces. Maybe not everyone will wake up. Maybe it's not necessary that they do. Does everyone in the family need to understand the damage caused to one family member who did come to remember these events, and let the rest just be? It's a difficult question. What if others in the family could benefit from having their innards shaken hard?"

Tension spread over the group. The questions Rachel asked surfaced in almost every meeting when someone revealed a hidden aspect of their lives, past or present. Avraham would not give unequivocal answers.

"It is my wish," he said in response, "that by the end of this year you'll each receive the answers you are hoping for. For years I've been both a clinical therapist and have run these courses so I can say that most people do come to an understanding which brings them peace of mind, although not necessarily forgiveness over the act itself that caused the damage. Despite the difficulties, people come to see that together we are one bolt of woven cloth, we are a matrix, a web of energy sending waves out to each other. I know that's a complex idea to consider."

Eva wondered to what degree people were indeed able to contain this perspective in light of their hardships, and especially because, as the book notes of the divine setting, everyone is a child of Shekhinah, everyone is born for the sake of good, and everyone deserves only good from the moment of birth. She also thought about how, as a whole, people are able to contain the understanding that 'I can escape from the world I see by giving up attack thoughts.' Of course that didn't mean escape through death, but through comprehension and an ambition for a better life.

"So why is there such terrible evil in the world?" she persisted, wanting an answer not only for herself but the entire group.

Avraham rubbed his temple. "Once we can sense the understanding in our bodies that everything is for the good, rather than try to understand it intellectually, we can accept that everything does turn out for our own good, that are souls are linked to each other's even before we come into this world. That will be the moment when we forgive. And again," he stressed, "we don't forgive the hurt caused. The damage has been done. It's tough, and painful. But we forgive that vibration of the soul by being aware that everything is for our good. That's exactly what studies in this course try to help us grasp, and that happens in a moment of enlightenment. You might be in the middle of a meeting and suddenly a deep sensation of tranquility spreads through your body. The pain will simply dissipate to a great degree. Even though it's there in your soul, you'll all testify to the fact that it's felt in a physical form."

At this stage it was still too difficult for the group to accept this idea but Avraham, gazing at them with his powerful, kind blue eyes, smiled at each person as though conveying a tremor of reassurance that they're in the right place with the right people at the right time.

It seemed to Eva that Avraham was not in quite as high spirits as usual. Nonetheless, the atmosphere was electric, perhaps because he decided to continue rather than call it a day. Or perhaps, Eva wondered, that was just her subjective perspective. The meeting was, for her, highly emotionally charged. She thought about the grandparents she'd never met because they were murdered in Auschwitz, as were her aunts and uncles. Nor had she ever seen a photo of her mother's family. She thought about Rachel: surrounded by family, living happily, and suddenly... what a terrible fissure to discover that the very people who should be protecting you are betraying their own grandchildren. She wondered what would drive parents to protect that one son despite the knowledge that he could be harming other children in their family.

Dozens of times Eva had listened to callers over the phone describing domestic sexual abuse. She had always tried to be there for those women, although sometimes it was men who called in. But it felt very different, very up close and personal, now that she could put a face to the voice.

Eva noted how Rachel's body hunched in on itself. She also noted the high necked clothing which conveyed understated elegance but actually served as a coverup. It clicked: why Rachel's shirts were never unbuttoned below the collar bone.

That was Rachel's subconscious way of guarding her body and soul. Suddenly Eva noticed that Rachel had undone the top button of her blouse, as though giving her neck space to breathe freely.

Eva couldn't stop thinking about the matrix of threads Avraham often spoke of, and how every person was connected to every other, even if unknowingly. She thought about how one person could damage another, or enable damage to take place, and how either impacted countless souls, directly or indirectly, along a narrative; how an account like the one the group had heard in this session would impact the listeners and echo further down, perhaps causing someone else to become aware, to realize a great harm or injury, even in seemingly normal families. This one story, she thought, can help others identify distress through body language, movements or words.

That led her to a possibly philosophical question: what exactly is 'normal'? How do we perceive success? Clothing? High ranking positions? How we are unconsciously less concerned when in the presence of such people? Eva recalled several well-known instances of individuals fitting those descriptions who turned out to be sexual predators, and how a slew and bevy of others stood up for them, talking about how much they contributed to their country and compatriots as though that cleared them of any responsibility for their actions. It infuriated her.

During her six years volunteering on the midnight to morning hotline shift, Eva had heard cases so horrific that she was unable to fall asleep once she got home. Hotline volunteers met monthly to receive psychological support to help them continue coping with the difficult situations they heard. In many cases, Eva and her colleagues knew they were there to listen: for the many women, and occasional man, who had the courage to phone in, the call was an outlet from evil. Nonetheless, she felt helpless: if not given specific permission, she couldn't phone the police, or have the offender removed from the environment in which the abuse was being carried out.

Perhaps her own pain, she thought, is easier to overcome in comparison to the pain recounted in Rachel's story. Rape or sexual abuse, both of which murder the soul and spirit, are no less impactful than actual murder.

The atmosphere was oppressive when the meeting ended. It was the severest narrative so far: incestual rape sears its way into body and mind for the rest of a person's life, leaving trauma that can never be fully overcome.

Betrayal is severe, but motherhood or fatherhood tainted by harm of this kind is far more acute. Many daunting life situations can be overcome: a person may learn to contain them, conceal or heal the wound. Sexual abuse injures the soul, the body, voids the self, a person's sense of sanctity. People who repress childhood abuse, which is later aroused in adulthood as a result of deeply buried memories forced to surface, experience physical pain, their hearts are torn to shreds, the mind cannot fathom the situation, and these impacts often lead to an array of illnesses that begin to rear their ugly head, derived from the long term suppression.

Children of victims of sexual attacks may suddenly come to understand events or links experienced in their childhoods: an absence of communication or of expressions of love towards them as children, indefinable fears, difficulties in maintaining sexual relationships, and reactions such as Rachel's: disgust of men with protruding bellies, being overly protective of their children, donning ultra-modest clothing to hide their body, and developing eating disorders, whether overeating or anorexia, to make the body undesirable.

Every trauma shapes us in some way but, to Eva, it seemed that the anguish that derives from sexual abuse was the hardest to live with and to reach some kind of forgiveness towards oneself. Some people experience early onset of dementia or

Alzheimer's when the memories suddenly surface and their brains cannot live with the consciousness of the event.

The very fact that Rachel shared her story was a dual shock for most of the group's members. A stigma exists where people assume that such actions occur only in poorly or uneducated families. Now the group was hearing a first-hand account of sexual abuse in an economically successful family of intelligent individuals, the kind of people others look up to, perceiving them to be worthy of emulation and learning from their success. Against what appeared to be a wonderful backdrop, horrifying rot had festered.

It raised questions once again about a person's environment, our families, the people we think we know until suddenly discovering behaviors we would never have associated with them.

Eva kept wondering about the phrases she read in the book: 'I am determined to see things differently' and 'I do not perceive my own best interests,' as well as 'I know what everything is for.'

Rachel repeatedly thanked the group for allowing and encouraging her to share her story. "I feel naked," she added with honest courage, "as though I've removed everything that covered me up my whole life. On one hand, that's a relief. I know it will all stay here in this room among us. On the other hand, it feels as though there's no space between my skin and the space around me, as though my body is dissolving."

"Actually, that's a good sign," Avraham said when Rachel paused, "because you no longer need that outer skin to protect you."

Back home, Eva couldn't stop thinking about Rachel and the rest of the group. No encounter is ever by chance, she acknowledged; not just for her but for everyone there.

In all honesty, she'd been considering discontinuing her volunteer activities on the nighttime hotline. She knew that her presence on the other end of the line was important to the women calling in, but she was feeling decidedly low on sources of inner strength to continue being a good listener. After this soul-jolting afternoon with Rachel, she realized just how important the listener's silence could be, when to say the right words, or contain the tears and sobs on the other end of the line. Right then she decided she'd continue volunteering after all.

CHAPTER 12

"My only function is the one God gave me."

Eva read the chapters Avraham had asked them to study. Would she find a statement, a word, recognize something in them that would help her come to terms with the group's previous meeting? 'I am not the victim of the world I see' and 'I have invented the world I see.' How does a person absorb that kind of statement? Does acknowledging it set us free? She could still sense her resistance to them, and sat down to write out several questions that she wanted to raise the next time the group met.

Instead of discussing the questions Eva had mentioned, Avraham chose to let Tamra share her story, asking Eva to write the questions on the flipchart. "We'll take a look at them later in the meeting, or the next time we meet," he added.

Tamra was pretty, multi-talented, a successful lawyer specializing in company mergers, but also a highly skilled multidisciplinary artist. She showed the group some of her work. Unable to decide where Tamra's greater talent lay, Eva wondered why she hadn't made art her primary occupation. At fifty-five, Tamra was a mother to three talented children, happily married to a hi-tech guy who loved her and supported everything she did. They lived in a beautiful private home in a prestigious neighborhood, traveled the world, and she enjoyed a multitude of friendships. In retrospect, everything was perfect. Of course, Eva was wondering what brought Tamra to the course.

When Tamra began speaking, it sounded as though she was talking to herself.

"Everything in my life's so perfect, even boringly so. Let's say it's too perfect. But in the past year, the more my parents aged, the more I started feeling that the time had come to do what I'd always wanted, but life hadn't allowed me. I wasn't supported in the one thing I truly wanted to be."

"I was an extremely creative child and, from a very young age, everyone realized that I'm an artist at heart, that I was born for it. But my parents, who ran a successful law firm, utterly rejected my request to study art, sculpting in clay, or any kind of artistic activity. As far as they were concerned, as their only child, my only choice of profession could be law and continuing the law firm they built with their own two hands.

"Deep inside, I opposed the idea but, as the only child, and because I was indeed scholastically gifted, at some point I just decided to give in to their wishes. I would secretly sketch, filling page upon page. I sketched at night, in school. I drew the teachers, the students, school life... but the artwork always stayed in my best friend Natalie's home.

"My parents were never happy with anything less than perfect grades. A ninety-five drew disparaging remarks, such as if only my head wasn't in the clouds I'd have gotten that hundred. I obeyed my parents' and the environment's codes of excellence.

"I only ever knew one grandmother, my father's mother. My maternal grandmother and both grandfathers passed away when I was too young to remember them. My paternal grandmother didn't support me either. I was so jealous of my friends, whose grandparents were their safe haven, where they could share their secrets. My grandmother was the type who has a subscription to the philharmonic orchestra where one wouldn't dare attend dressed in jeans, as we've more recently seen. I also happily took out a subscription.

"My grandmother also read literature, not your everyday bestsellers. Her friends were doctors and lawyers, managers of successful companies and so on. She always dressed elegantly, but jeans was a forbidden item. It's also how my parents lived, and I felt trapped, living in a bubble of deceit.

"One day Natalie's mother found the sketches and asked who they belonged to but, when Natalie told her our secret, Natalie's mother hugged me warmly and said that I'm the most talented person she's ever met and that my secret will stay safe with her, although she'd love it if I wanted to show her other works in the future. And that's how Natalie's mother, Aya, became part of the secret.

"You can't imagine," Tamra said, pausing momentarily, "how relieved I was. But keeping this secret from my parents exacted its price. I developed all kinds of imaginary illnesses. For example, I'd get a temperature out of nowhere, just to get some unconditional attention and warmth from them without having to balance that with some kind of excellence. I missed a lot of school, both in lower and higher grades, but still managed to pass with top marks.

"I was about sixteen when I decided to forego on the art. I realized it would only hurt my parents. I asked Natalie, with whom I stayed close over the years, to store my work at her place, and she did.

"I finished high school with honors and, to my parents' and grandmother's joy, was accepted into the military career track program in law. As expected, it was one accolade after another. Slowly the art bug faded, or so I thought. During my Master's studies I met my husband, also from an affluent family and who was brought up in a similar socio-economic framework. He's very good looking, charming, my soul mate, and also an only child. Our parents, who only met once we decided to marry, became the closest of friends.

"My husband's in hi-tech. He, like me, was always expected to excel so, as soon as he graduated with honors, of course, because how not! he started working with computers. Eventually he and two study mates established a successful cyber company. Unsurprisingly both of us wanted a larger than one-child family.

"I had difficulties becoming pregnant but treatment brought about our twins, a boy and a girl. Three years later, we had another daughter. We were so pleased, and promised ourselves that our kids would never be raised under that threatening whip called excellence. And yet, despite our emotional closeness, I never told my husband about my artistic side, mostly because it was so repressed.

"Eventually I took over management of my parents' law firm, which did very well. I employ ten lawyers, the office is considered number one here for labor contracts, I live a really good life with a lovely home, a new car every three years, and three talented kids who we let be a bit mischievous, not allowing ourselves to make waves about their mix of great and average grades.

"Two years ago when our youngest, a redhead and real charmer, turned ten, she made a gift for the family. It was wrapped in beautiful paper and bore gold lettering. 'To Mother and Father, and my beloved bro Ido and sis Ayelet, a gift from me.' Slowly, carefully, we opened it to find an absolutely stunning oil painting in the hyper-realist style. It was a portrait of the family standing in a circle in the desert with an amazing sunset background.

"Each of us is drawn in the minutest detail, but also with something of each one's character coming through. Ido, Ayelet, and my husband Adam stood in complete shock. I froze, then burst into heaving sobs. No one understood what was happening. Ilana, our sweet little girl, came over to hug me. It was clear to everyone that I was crying with utter joy. But no one could imagine what else hid behind my tears.

"We were so happy at this birthday party. I was floating. Adam realized I was going through something and asked me about it. I said that everything was fine and asked everyone not to make plans for the following night because I had a surprise.

"The next morning I called Natalie and told her about Ilana's painting. She laughed and said that Ilana had come to them asking for help buying the canvas stretched on a frame and the oil paints, because she wanted it to be a big surprise. Natalie was happy to back her up. I asked Natalie to come over with her husband and kids that evening. Hers were born around the same times as mine so they all grew up like siblings. And I asked her to bring my secret treasure box.

"That evening she arrived with her family, which was a very natural event in our home, especially when it came to one of our children's birthdays. She came in with a beautiful red leather carry folder, which she'd bought as a gift for me long ago to store my artwork.

"She looked around. 'Okay,' she announced, 'the moment of truth for your mother has come. Now you'll understand where Ilana's amazing talent has come from.' And with that she opened my folder and let the artwork spill onto our large glass dining table. In one instant, all my work up to the age of sixteen was revealed for the very first time. My family looked at the work, amazed. Adam came over and hugged me tightly.

"Then he looked at me with his head cocked slightly to one side. 'I must say,' he said, gazing at me, 'that I'm really upset. Your entire life you've kept your love of painting and art hidden from me. What I mean is, okay, we all know you're a gallery trawler, an art collector, but suddenly we see why!'

"Once the initial excitement died down after Ilana picked up one page after another, happy, laughing, realizing where her amazing talent is from, we all sat down to a great meal. I told everyone how my parents simply didn't see art as anything but inferior, that it would never provide me with a profession, it won't keep my feet firmly on the ground, as they used to say. And that's when it hit me. I've got to get back to my artwork. I've pushed it aside for too many years. So that's what I started doing.

"I delegated the office's management to one of our most talented lawyers, rented a studio to work, and began painting almost non-stop like a crazed woman. I painted on canvases, one after the other, I started sketching, photographing, sculpting in clay. Then one day my parents came to the office, as they do on occasion, and saw a different name on my office door. Puzzled, they phoned me right away. I told them not to get upset, everything's fine, I'm still head of the office but I asked them to hop into a taxi and come to my studio address without saying a word about why.

"A short while later there was a hesitant knock on the door of my spacious place in a classic Tel Aviv Bauhaus-style building, with those massive windows and high ceilings, and the small balconies overlooking a charming inner courtyard. They stood in the doorway, in stunned silence.

"And me, I was in a track suit, not a messy frayed one but nonetheless, very non-aristocratic looking," Tamra chuckled, "with splotches of colorful paint all over it and me radiating happiness; Adam and our children there too, gazing round. My parents stood there as though fossilized. Maybe it was the paintings, or maybe the fact that my husband and kids were there too, I couldn't say. Perhaps a bit of each. Maybe they realized that, you can guide the girl away from the art, but you can't take the art out of the girl.

"My kids ran to their grandparents. It's interesting but, since they retired my parents have softened, spending more and more time with the children. They'd been following Ilana's artistic development and were very proud of her, but had never told her about their own daughter's artistic skills.

"The gut punch over, the children pulled them from room to room, each filled with oil paintings of almost every style, as though I just wanted to experience everything at once to make up for all the lost time. Despite my success as a lawyer, something had never been whole. I'd always carried a longing. To paint, of course. And the only release I'd allowed myself was to make pencil sketches in the courtroom or sometimes in long meetings which were so dull that a colleague would give me a small kick under the table to bring my attention back to the issue at hand. That's when I'd sketch miniatures of the people present, or draw some abstract form.

"So my parents wandered around the works, and then made another round, and eventually they got to my school folder and paged through the artwork. Then they said the most wonderful words I've ever heard. 'We're so proud of you!' What an uplift that was! I hugged them so tight and burst into tears. And my cold, distanced mother who'd never shed a tear in public burst into tears too, and actively hugged me back.

"My parents were genuinely so thrilled that they promised to help arrange an exhibition. Most importantly, at the exhibition they would tell their story and share their insights about how parents shouldn't trample their children's talents and dreams, nor try to turn their own children into reflections of themselves.

"I imagine that right now you're asking yourselves," Tamra continued in a voice that implied she was sharing a secret, "if everything's turned out so great, why on earth is she here? Having had my talent castrated for so many years, I still have frequent moments when I think that maybe I really am better at being a lawyer than an artist, and this childlike lack of confidence is leading me into blind spots. I need so much reinforcement.

"I asked my parents not to interfere, not to arrange a showing, not to make use of the friend who owns a gallery. They were a bit peeved but, to their credit, they stepped aside. I decided to sign the artwork, even though up until then I hadn't put my signature on anything. So I added dates and a classy literary name. I wanted to send photos of my work to galleries under a name they wouldn't identify me with to see if my work had any value. I chose the name Koti, which is the short form of my late grandfather's name.

"I hired an expert in photographing artwork and began sending the photos to various galleries. But I did that only after joining this class and sitting here facing you, Avraham, and hearing what others have been through. I realized how incredibly lucky I've been, and decided to jump in at the deep end and, along the way, also forgive my parents. I needed to understand why it was so important for them to suppress my love of art when it was clear I had more than average talent.

"About a week later, an invitation came back from one of Tel Aviv's top galleries. 'Please bring your paintings. We look forward to meeting you.' They proposed a solo exhibition, along with an offer to be my agent.

"Last week, after Rachel shared her difficult narrative, I called and told my parents I wanted to meet with them, just the three of us. They received me warmly and we sat down in their extravagant living room, stylized by a top designer who works with elite society but which, to me, is uninviting and lacks warmth. They've lived in their current apartment for only a couple of years, having left the huge private home that was just too big for them.

"But they are in a very spacious twenty-fifth floor apartment with stunning views across all Tel Aviv, the sea, and all the way out to the horizon. The thing about my parents' place, which is important for that strata of society, is that every visitor knows where everything was bought and how much they forked out for it. Four large-scale wall paintings of mine are hung there, as well as three naïve style paintings by my daughter, Ilana.

"Well, I sat down facing them, looked around, and asked a tiny yet huge question: why?

"They gazed at each other and suddenly I noticed a tear on my mother's cheek, and another on my father's. And then they took a huge breath and began to talk.

"Grandfather Peter, my mother's father, was a renowned artist in Paris during the 1930s and 40s. He was a friend of Georges Braque, Picasso, and many others of the period. It was a time when rules about painting, architecture and fashion were being thrown out the window, and women were increasingly wearing trousers, emulating Coco Chanel. And it was a time of wild parties, can-can clubs and so on. My grandmother came from a very wealthy family, fell in love with Peter, and they married.

"My grandmother's parents weren't in favor of the marriage because Peter was, well, poor, but over time they got to know his personality and saw that their daughter was truly happy with her husband. He began selling his work, aided by his wife's affluent family, and then black clouds began rolling into Europe. Antisemitism spread further and further, but my grandfather was certain that, by virtue of his friendship with the period's greatest artists and thinkers, he wouldn't be affected by it. My grandmother's parents began pressuring them to leave Paris and immigrate to the Holy Land. At the time, they lived in Berlin and my great grandfather owned a factory. They were planning on leaving, and insisted that my grandmother, their daughter, join them but Grandfather Peter wouldn't agree to board the boat. He gave my grandmother some two dozen paintings rolled up in a suitcase and promised that in another few months he'd see how matters were developing and join them.

"But far less than a few months later was already too late. The Nazis invaded Paris and my grandfather discovered that his artist friends wouldn't even help find him somewhere to hide. He was deeply disappointed to see that no one came to his aid when the SS knocked on his studio's door, behaved like thugs and tore up all his work other than a few that an officer, not knowing that my grandfather understood German, asked to set aside. Then they handcuffed and beat him, and he was sent to Auschwitz where he was murdered after first being forced to paint a family portrait for the Auschwitz concentration camp's commander.

"My grandmother learned of her husband's murder only after the war. She turned inwards like a snail retracting to its shell, diving into the aristocratic lifestyle she'd so strongly shunned as a teen."

"My parents fell silent, and came over to me with tears in their eyes and embraced me lovingly in a way I'd never before experienced. 'We hope you understand now,' they said. 'Every beautiful painting you produced stabbed at grandmother's heart like a dagger. We decided to protect her soul but the price hurt your soul.' In that instant I was so sorry my grandmother was no longer alive. I wanted to take her hand and tell her that I understand."

Tamra's eyes scanned the group. She smiled warmly. "My first exhibition opens this coming weekend. I chose to dedicate it to my grandfather," Tamra announced with evident happiness as Eva realized why it had been so important for Avraham to let Tamra be this meeting's focus. "And it's because of you all," Tamra added. "Because of this group, my grandfather will receive at least some of his due credit.

"When the gallery's owners heard my story and saw my

grandfather's paintings, they were incredibly excited. They knew about him. Perhaps my grandmother hoped that one day her husband's works would be seen, which is why she kept them under lock and key for all those years. The paintings were perfectly preserved and will be positioned at the exhibition's entrance, followed by my daughter's work, and then mine."

While Tamra spoke a tense silence prevailed. It spoke of mystery, excitement and a sense of hope. The group felt strong partnership with this unique event: a three generational showing of works by a grandfather, granddaughter and great-granddaughter.

"I hope," Tamra added, "that by the end of this year I'll be at peace with my choice and perhaps understand that I can be both artist and lawyer without any conflict between the two, and that one doesn't come at the cost of the other."

Later, walking into her home, Eva gazed around at the artwork she'd purchased over the years, as well as works she herself had painted when younger. Who can know what hides behind every brush stroke and color, or the name of a painting! She smiled.

It was no surprise that Eva loved art. She'd taken art courses simultaneous to her work as a designer and architect. She suddenly noticed that she'd begun studying the works in her home, and in galleries and museums, from a new perspective. Because of Tamra's story perhaps?

She paid particular attention to works by Edward Gerstein, now deceased but who she and her husband had supported when he came to live in Israel. In return, he gifted them abstract paintings which adorned her home. One evening she sat in front of one of Gerstein's paintings, focused on lines of words hidden among the reds and crimsons, maroons and yellows. Pushkin: Edward himself had told her that the words were from Pushkin. She decided to find someone who could translate them for her.

Tamra's exhibition opened that weekend. Of course the group turned up en-masse, hugging and congratulating her, meeting her parents, her children, and Natalie, who took care of Tamra's paintings all these years too, replicating a similar family secret. They also met Tamra's staff who now worked under the direction of a thrilled, easy-going lawyer who gave them plenty of freedom inside and outside the office.

Eva had brought one of her clients, for whom she had just completed plans for an office block, to the showing. The boardroom needed a special piece of art. Special, he explained, meant something with an interesting backstory. He purchased two wonderful pieces of art. To Eva it felt like coming full circle: a wonderful family with a secret that slowly comes to light, much like the company for which she planned the office space, its vision and work aiming for openness and closeness among the staff and the staff's families.

Who can imagine what else these artworks might bring about? Perhaps one day, Eva thought, they'll inspire someone else with a secret passion.

CHAPTER 13

"My only function is the one God gave me."

A pleasant atmosphere was evident at the next session's start. Most conversations centered around Tamra's story, simultaneously holding so much pain yet also so much hope and optimism.

Avraham began by scanning everyone, his blue eyes always reminding Eva of her father's. Something about that particular shade of blue made her wonder if it gave the person a unique ability to delve into depths without feeling whelmed by the negative factors in the world. Avraham studied Sarai and smiled.

"Would you like to share what you've experienced and what's weighing on your heart now?" he asked. "Remember, Emily also kept silent, just like you, but came around to sharing her story. We haven't heard from you yet. Ready?"

A pretty, tall, slim woman in her sixties, Sarai conveyed an impression of seriousness, rarely smiling. Dark brown hair was cut to envelope her face, reminiscent to some degree of Audrey Hepburn. She usually sat with one leg crossed over the other, barely moving or changing position, almost as though frozen in time.

When Eva opened her eyes during meditation, she always noticed that Sarai's eyes were open. Eva also had trouble with meditation sometimes, especially when the sessions were longer. She felt a need to look around, and was relieved when Avraham said it was okay for them to occasionally open their eyes, promising that over time it would become much easier to keep them closed and feel safe and secure.

Sarai breathed deeply. She began talking in a tone that sounded like she was telling someone else's narrative.

"I read the lines 'My only function is the one God gave me' and 'I would fulfill my function that I may be happy' and that both come from the same source. If I want to find happiness, I need to learn how to identify what makes me happy. I thought about what actually brought me to these meetings. I am not spiritual-minded in the least, or so I believe. I've never read anything that isn't down-to-earth, nor have I ever connected with anything but the practical, the commonsensical. I don't believe in reincarnation and all that silly stuff of souls choosing to be born into the world via this or that family for the sake of undergoing some process. From my point of view, we're born, we live here, we die here. That's it. Bye-bye and never see you again. I don't believe in spiritual communication, or any kind of healing with someone who isn't a doctor and doesn't use modern medicine."

Sarai's admission took the group by surprise, particularly in light of the course title specifically relating to miracles and the material they were reading which came, presumably, via spiritual communication. Yet here Sarai was, and continued to be.

"How'd you hear about the course?" Avraham asked.

"I was sitting at the hair salon and two women were talking about you," Sarai answered, smiling. "They were detailing the course and how it changed their lives. Since I often get bored and can't find what to do with myself, I decided I had nothing to lose. Nor did I have anything particularly exciting on the drawing board. I had no clue what the course was about and, in fact, I was pretty concerned when I heard that it was a one-year commitment.

"But then, without understanding what motivated me, I phoned and you suggested we meet. And I have no clue what happened to me," she added, smiling again, "but something in the way you talked, or your gaze, or your manner, just enchanted me. I didn't even think about what I want from this course, or why I'm registering. I just said that I would, and here I am.

"Then I started reading the book at home and my whole world flipped. The words undermined everything I'd ever thought or believed. My partner doesn't understand what's going on, nor do my kids, or grandchildren. I have a large family: four children, two girls who became religiously observant, and each has five children. They're both very successful. One's a psychologist, the other's in real estate. Their husbands work in hi-tech even though they're ultra-Orthodox.

"And my two sons, each with two children. They're also hi-techers, and their wives are truly sweet. I love them both. One decided to be a fulltime mother, like me, and the other runs a small but very unique fashion studio with a permanent customer base. She chooses her fabrics very carefully: organic cottons that take into account the ecological footprint in their production. She's vegan, unsurprisingly. We meet a lot as a family, especially since most of them live fairly close to us, and their parents. In short, it all looks so wonderful. What's there to complain about? And if it's okay to say, I'm also a pretty good cook."

"Of course you can say so. It's even valuable to tell us that!" different group members responded.

"So I'm sitting here and listening to your life stories and feeling like a total idiot, if you'll pardon me. But that's the feeling I've had ever since my kids flew the coop, and even more so since my husband retired and began wandering about, getting in my way, and then decided to join a cooking course to 'realize himself' and, in the process took over the only spot where I had control and, let's say, ownership."

Sarai stopped, smoothing down her shirt. Then she rolled

her sleeves up and opened a couple of buttons. "Wow, I've gotten warm," she smiled. "Well, about a year ago we bought a new place that would better suit our lives: fewer rooms, but a larger kitchen area which we decided to keep kosher so that our orthodox girls and their families would be fully comfortable, assured that the Jewish laws relating to keeping kosher are fully observed at all times. There's ample space for a very large dining table to fit everyone in together, a roomy living area, a main bedroom with ensuite bathroom, which we'd never had before, and two rooms for the grandkids. We wanted a large balcony overlooking sea views as a calm place for breakfasts and afternoon coffee and so on. Our retirement apartment.

"But, from the moment that we started planning, my husband decided that he knows better than I what we need in the kitchen, and I felt choked. We moved in, I purchased lovely new furnishings, we hung the paintings we'd bought over the years but, from the second that we unpacked all our boxes, I felt like I was being boxed in. My husband blossomed. He went to courses, he cooked, he tried out all kinds of workshops. I, on the other hand, felt like I was withering from one day to the next. I wondered if this was depression. I didn't want to get up in the morning. I didn't want to visit the grandkids, who were always happy when I came. I didn't want to meet friends, go to cafés. Suddenly it hit me, and made me anxious for the daughter-in-law who chose to be a homemaker like me, rather than realize her amazing abilities in the world of graphic art.

"So there I sat in my spacious home, looking around, my kids grown up and gone, my husband retired, and me? I had no function anymore," she said, swallowing hard and halting momentarily. "I'd been a top level student in high school, mostly in sciences. I'd planned to enlist, do my military service, then study physics or chemistry, two areas I really loved. But in my last year of high school I met the man who'd become my husband. He'd just completed his military service and had started working with air conditioning systems. He went to advanced workshops and I missed him. I was blinded by love.

"He was so pleasant and polite, from a good family, and my parents also fell in love with him instantly. My father wasn't crazy about me recruiting, then studying a 'male' subject such as physics or chemistry, but I insisted. It's just that some months later, my husband proposed. To this day I have no idea if my parents had a hand in the matter. They're no longer alive so I have no one to confront. I did ask my husband but he says there was no such thing.'

"Our wedding was lively, happy. I was among the first in my circle of friends to marry, a fraction before my nineteenth birthday. At twenty I was already a mother and all my dreams of physics or chemistry had evaporated. The only chemistry I got to know really well was what my kids left in their diapers," Sarai smiled. "When I wanted to go and study, my husband said it'd be a problem because who, he asked, would look after the kids? He traveled around the country a lot, came home late every day, became increasingly proficient in his field of large scale air conditioning systems for buildings, and did really well. I put all of myself into mothering, cooking, play-dates for the kids. But there was a constant background message in my mind: just a bit longer, the kids will be grown, I can go and study. If not physics or chemistry, some profession that would enhance my life.

"Days rolled on, one after the other. One son enlisted and I got all into being the soldier's-mother, a worry bug. Then a daughter enlisted. Then our other son. Then our youngest daughter. And the feeling never goes away: that my life is just slipping between my fingers and I still haven't completely understood how that happened. One morning I woke up and just said, 'Enough! I've got to do something for myself!' The trouble was that I had no idea anymore what. I felt I could use some help, realizing that not everything had to be based solely on the material, and that maybe there was something to all this new age stuff that everyone was talking about, that it was time to peer out beyond my shell, and start living. So far I've lived alongside life, but I don't want that anymore."

"And then that hair salon incident happened. My husband, who's used to me being what's usually known as 'the little woman' doesn't understand what's going on with me. I come along and drive him crazy with statements like 'a chair isn't a chair' and questions about 'who am I' and then a course in spiritual communication, and he's convinced I've gone mad."

Everyone smiled understandingly at that.

"But as the days go by, I see what I've missed out on and am panicked at that I could continue missing had I not woken up on time. Suddenly, instead of being angry with husband for taking over the kitchen, I say thanks to him every morning. Thanks, because that's what shook me up. My friends call but suddenly I'm busy. With what? I don't really know, other than the fact that they don't interest me so much anymore. I don't have the patience to forward and tweet and ooh and aah about the grandkids, and clothes, and cooking.

"Now I wake in the morning, meditate, and generally don't understand how I got where I am. I just know that inside I'm beaming. Even though I still don't quite know why I'm here in this course, or where it will lead me, I do know for the first time after many, many years that I'm in the company of people who are interesting, who make me feel good, and who arouse my curiosity.

"So, science still appeals to me, it's still my big love, but what can I do about that as a senior citizen? Maybe this course will help me find my path. Currently I'm just bumbling around, fumbling, feeling my way, but not entirely in the darkness. My children sense changes. So do the grandkids. They're supportive. They say that since leaving the kitchen behind, I have much more vitality. I started showing interest in my grandchildren's science studies, helping them a bit, too. I bought an iPhone, an iPad and a laptop, and am getting the hang of it all so fast that everyone's been taken by surprise, especially me.

"Suddenly things have turned around. My husband is the chef, and I've become the technology person at home. It's funny, and gives rise to many thoughts about our paths over the years, and what actually directs us, our decisions, our choices.

"I wonder: was cooking always my husband's dream but back then, men didn't do that so much, they didn't run the kitchen at home the way women did, just as women didn't go and study physics? Yes, there are always those trailblazers, and I salute them with admiration! I wasn't one of them. I followed a known and unsurprising path," Sarai continued, the words coming smoothly. "What should I feel? Frustration? Anger? At whom? Maybe only towards myself? On the other hand, did we think any differently back then?

"I hear your life stories and even though some of them aren't simple, they hone the message that failure can actually be an extremely powerful catalyst and especially, the understanding that life simply flowed by, and I hardly intervened. I followed circumstances, and even though I understand that it was my choice to do so, it's hard for me to accept that I'm at fault for that."

"I'm now reading numerous books related to spirituality, trying to see where I'm headed. When I began this course I was afraid I might already have missed the last bus, so to speak, but no, that's not true. Feeling without taking action is also a choice, but this time, I've decided to make different choices. It's like Eva said: dreams have no expiration date.

"I'm going to check into studies on trading and share markets. That's a combination of math, probability, the unknown, and some element of risk. Maybe now's the time to take some of the money I put aside from selling my parents' home to study an adrenalin pumping subject!"

Sarai was becoming visibly excited and, as a result, short of breath. "Take a moment, Sarai, take a few sips of water," Avraham advised, smiling. She nodded, and followed his suggestion.

"About a month after the course started," Sarai continued, "I started reading the financial newspapers. I swapped out my regular women's magazine full of items on cooking and celebs gossip for a completely different reading framework, the kind that business people read, and I must say that it made me feel great. My husband says that as long as it involves the money from my parents and not our joint account, I should go ahead, have some fun, as he put it.

"I know, it's a pretty demeaning attitude on his part, and he jokes about it in front of the kids and our friends, saying things like 'Sarai's turning into an economist.' At first I was hurt, insulted, but the longer I'm in this course and absorbing the ideas it proffers, the more I see it's his self-defense system talking and it has nothing to do with me. It's his need to justify the revolution I'm experiencing, and that's his way of coping. It's not pleasant, I have to admit. Initially, with every belittling or mocking comment, I cringed inside and went back to being 'the little woman,' but slowly, in reaction to his remarks and mocking attitude, I'm growing more persistent, telling him I'm making some nice money and that it's a fascinating field where I'm learning so much.

"Our friends just don't get it: Sarai the cook, the mother, the grandma, the wife, has suddenly started talking about shares and explaining economic procedures! But I'm also slowly seeing that they're listening to me and female friends come to consult with me about money they've put aside for a rainy day. I'm beginning to feel ready to start working in the field, and toying with the idea that I could specialize in a specific area and become a salaried broker, even if only part time."

"Maybe we'll all consult with you about our money!" Emily interjected.

Eva noticed that Sarai's legs were no longer crossed. She had both feet on the floor and sat very upright in her chair. The slouch that had broadcast 'I am nothing' had been replaced with firm, stable posture and a smile that signaled the start of Sarai's victory.

"I will never forget the moment I opened a bank account for myself," Eva mentioned. "I remember it because I was staring at my name on the check book. I sat there with our banker, who taught me the basics of account management. It was such an uplifting feeling, even though I was alone. But it meant control over my own life. I realized that any decisions I made, for better or worse, would be totally my own."

"I can connect with what you've just said," Sarai agreed. "That was exactly how I felt when I set up an appointment at the bank and asked to redeem funds I had closed up in an account that only my husband made decisions over as a matter of course. I simply went with him to sign documents, without having a clue how long the deposit was set for, what its conditions were, and so on. In fact, it never really occurred to me to ask. Why would the 'little woman' need to bother her pretty head with that kind of information? But now I've decided to go to an investment company and learn how to become a smart investor.

"It probably sounds a bit silly, but I even bought a suit for the occasion. It made me feel important, independent. Actually, I did the opposite of you, Eva. You dropped your constantly formal clothes for skinny jeans and layered tops. And the opposite of you too, Tamra. You swapped your elegant representational clothing for comfy things to get dirty in at the studio. By contrast, I now feel it's time for me to wear business attire. You're both already earned respect in your fields. Now it's my turn to dress the part and prove myself. Maybe the day will come when I'll put my tailored outfits aside but, for now, they do make me feel that I'm in sync with what I'm doing.

"I'm learning from this course, and from all of you. I know

that when I'm at peace with myself, with who I am, with my past, present and unknowable future, I'll be able to wear a sexy dress and people will nonetheless take me seriously rather than consider me transparent, particularly my husband. The literature I'm reading, and will keep reading, stresses that everything depends on how I feel about myself, that external appearances are no more than that, but I hope that you'll understand if next week I show up in a tailored suit... " she ended, a broad smile lighting up her face.

The meeting was over. Back in her car, the words Avraham had once said to her as she entered the room popped into her mind. "One day your place will be this chair I'm currently sitting on." Confidence flooded her. Suddenly Eva realized how her story had influenced the other women. In fact, everyone's story had an impact on each of the other members in the group, but Eva knew inside that she was at the threshold of something new and, despite the difficulties she was experiencing, her journey would help many other women, and men, through crises in their personal lives, in their intimate relationships, in their employment interactions, in their family connections.

As soon as she arrived home, she opened the safe and pulled out a folder with banking documents. Then she picked up her check books, which still bore her and her husband's names. For some reason, even though that joint account was no longer active, she hadn't destroyed them. Down in the garden she cleared a small space and dropped them there along with several other documents which she knew she'd no longer need. Among them were photos of 'the other woman.' She'd found her husband's stash. Down on her knees, she gazed at the pile, lit a fire, sighed with immense relief, and thanked the cosmos and Sarai's story.

CHAPTER 14

"Today in gratitude we lift our hearts above despair,
and raise our thankful eyes,
no longer looking downward to the dust."

This meeting would be the last before the three-week Passover break. Sarai walked into the very ordinary room with its neon ceiling lights wearing an emerald-green suit, which beautifully contoured her slim body, and high heels. She simply filled the room with her presence. The downtrodden air which had encompassed her demeanor had disappeared. Hardly transparent? Hardly likely! That was Eva's immediate thought.

Sarai wasn't the only one radiating satisfaction. Sharon, who'd insisted on being called 'Shereene' was already seated. Sharon, who had come late to every meeting so far, had never participated in the start when Avraham had gazed at each person there, and had never joined the group for meditation. In all honesty, her behavior annoyed everyone.

Shereene-Sharon was tall, with very long, beautiful legs and powerful thighs, very evident when she wore tights. She wasn't pretty in the classic sense. Her facial features were out of proportion: relatively small eyes, slightly slanted; a straight, Nordic nose which made Eva think of her own; protruding cheeks above a full mouth which made Eva wonder if the effect was achieved by artificial means. Sharon's long flowing hair was streaked blond and auburn and she constantly fiddled with it.

Most striking was her pair of large sunglasses, its frame black, its lenses very dark, much in the trademark style of high priestess of fashion and Vogue magazine manager, Anna Wintour. Despite Wintour's renown for making or breaking fashion icons and styles virtually instantly, Eva had always wondered about those sunglasses: were they a look-at-me reveal or a don't-look-too-deeply conceal?

Eyes say so much about a person, that much was clear to Eva, especially after people she worked with closely told her that her eyes had stopped smiling. She thought about her iridology course. That eyes could be the source of diagnoses for the entire body had never ceased to amaze her.

Shereene's eyes were always hidden by glasses for short-sightedness. Their lenses were darker than regular ones. Dressed in an avant-garde style, the broad brimmed hat she wore no matter what the weather was like also shaded her eyes. Her style included plenty of colorful jewelry items that clinked and rattled whenever she moved. Four rings adorning her fingers were set with diamonds, amber, rubies and amethysts. In short: she couldn't be missed wherever she went. And no less so when she walked in late to join the group.

Avraham was also taken by surprise but he smiled warmly at Shereene as though he was in on her secret.

As always, the meeting began with Avraham gazing at each of them. But this time, Shereene removed her dark-lensed glasses. Meditation began. It was longer than usual, and focused on the third eye, at Avraham's request.

"What is your third eye gazing at? Or perhaps avoiding?" he asked, the question filling the room. "Do we have the ability to use it when our seeing eyes are closed?"

The meditation over, Avraham asked Shereene if she'd like to speak. She, who frequently interjected in others' conversations and was always free with advice but wouldn't listen to any herself, lowered her head, removed her hat and quietly, unlike her usual rowdy tone, said, "Yes," and began her story.

"I was abroad with my partner and another two couples, very close friends. We flew to Cannes, booked rooms at the most luxurious hotel, as we usually do. This time it was the International Carlton, built in 1909 and considered a national historic structure by the French government. It's where you meet film stars and, in particular, Arab sheikhs. The really rich ones. The day after we arrived, I was walking along the beautiful promenade with my two girlfriends and we stopped next to a shopping area that sells only high-end brands. Jewelry. Clothing. Shops we'd been into not once, not twice but any number of times with our husbands."

Shereene clasped and unclasped her hands, sighed, and continued. "We stood at the display window of the Italian shoe company, Pollini. I was studying a gorgeous pair of sandals in a stunning bluish turquoise snakeskin on a high heel, the way I love my shoes."

Eva thought about her sister who also loved very high heels and the way the two of them would walk for miles in New York, Eva in sports shoes and her sister on stilettos. Her sister's ability to do that always made Eva jealous. As little girls they'd travel to Tel Aviv with their mother and visit their cousins. Aunt Aggie was married to Eva's maternal uncle, who was much older than his wife. They always played with Auntie Aggie's shoes. That's when Eva's sister gained her stiletto balancing skills, and never seemed to tire no matter how much they walked.

"Those sandals were just beckoning me," Shereene smiled. "You know that feeling, right?" Some nodded. "That's how I always bought clothes. Impulsively. My friends urged me on. 'Go in! Try them on!' but I held back, looking around, feeling a bit embarrassed because I suddenly realized I didn't have my husband's credit card on me and the cash budget he gave me that morning wouldn't be enough. 'I don't have my credit card,' I said to one of my friends in a whisper, but they didn't understand. 'What do you mean, you don't have a credit card?' They were puzzled. 'Did you forget it at the hotel? Lose it?' And again I whispered my answer. 'I don't have one of my own and the cash my husband gave me this morning isn't enough, because I was too tired to have sex with him.' They were shocked."

"They told me afterwards that they felt as though they'd been hit by a bomb. They looked at me, unbelieving. It had never occurred to them that the elegant prestigious black card in my purse wasn't my own but only had my husband's name on it. Nor did it ever occur to them that the amount of cash I had in my pocket, that my husband gave me, depended on how I conducted myself; how my behavior towards this charming, friendly man who tossed money about without batting an eyelid determined how much money I had on any particular day.

"Then they started recalling details that, before then, had much less meaning to them: situations where he held my hand too tightly, actually gripping my hand to make me go where he was going. Or lorded it over me, hugging me not from love and generosity but ownership. They couldn't fathom that I didn't have my own credit card and money of my own, especially since we both came from affluent families. That's when they also understood the dark glasses in black frames that became an inseparable part of my look but were there to hide my shame, my fear of being caught out."

Her eyes downcast, feeling uncomfortable, Shereene fingered the glasses she was holding in her hand before continuing her story. "These glasses... they're not prescription lenses. They're just dark glass meant to cover the window into my soul," she winced. "I could never anticipate what sort of situation might come up and whether I could handle it, which made me anxious and so ashamed. These women, who began as my friends since the day I married only because their husbands were my husband's friends from his university days, were left speechless. They gazed at me, until one of them, Shira, realized how uncomfortable the situation was and hugged me. 'We'll get through this with you,' she said. 'We'll help you.' They promised that they wouldn't say a word of what happened that day to their husbands, until I felt the time was ripe."

"A few days later we flew back to our home and our three children, who I'm so proud of and love so much. They're the most precious things I have, really. I hugged each of them very tight, which they're not really used to because they grew up with a nanny who gave them all the warmth they needed. Right then I decided that I need to switch my life around altogether, go to therapy, figure myself out, understand why I let this situation develop, and recalibrate my life trajectory. As you probably noticed, I'm fairly opiniated. Well, perhaps a bit more than fairly, and I'm always late," she said, giving another wincing smirk, "because it's important for me to be last in, and perhaps when everyone gazes at me making my entrance, it's meant to compensate for the attention I don't get at home.

"In any event, the day after we were back I called the psychologist that my wonderful friends recommended. They pooled the money together for me for therapy to prevent my husband from asking questions. One day the light bulb moment came. It was a terrible moment, frightening and simultaneously awakening, and every descriptor you could possibly imagine, all at once. I realized that I'm the second generation of financial abuse. Suddenly I remembered shopping bags my mother would secretly bring into the house so that 'your father doesn't see them,' I remembered her little cash purse which never held a credit card because she used to said that 'credit cards are for the youngsters and, anyway, I don't need such silliness because I could never figure how to work the bank's credit machine.' She meant the ATM, of course."

Right then Eva's throat closed tightly. She started to cough hard, repeatedly, and couldn't calm herself. Her reaction embarrassed her as all attention turned towards her. Picking up her water bottle, she quickly drank.

"Sorry about that," Eva said "but I'll admit I was also afraid of the ATM," she eventually managed to blurt. "I did have credit cards and never needed to justify my purchases but, in a really stupid way, my husband would leave me the cash I needed. Only after he left, I stood there in front of the machine for the first time, feeling scared and brave, and withdrew cash from what seemed like a 'money dispenser' that provides cash night and day."

Emily nodded in empathy. Perhaps the pause that Eva's coughing and explanation caused was nonetheless of value, allowing Shereene to take a breath and the atmosphere to lighten a little.

Shereene smiled and nodded at Eva, too, in understanding. "In that therapy session I was sure I was going to collapse. I understood that I'd chosen a husband who was a copy of my father. A successful businessman. Handsome and well-dressed. Someone whose every wish must be fulfilled. Until that point, I'd never seen how my mother was in exactly the same position then that I was in now. My mother passed away some years ago from throat cancer but now, sitting and sharing everything with you," she laughed, tossing her hair back, "well, almost everything, if I'm being honest... "

Shereene paused, gathering her thoughts. Eva wondered what else she might be concealing.

"In any event," Shereene continued, "now I understand why my mother's cancer started in her throat. She couldn't make her voice heard. Her voice was silenced for all those years while she was living 'happily ever after,' as people concluded from the image they were presented. My father, heartbroken at her death, quickly found a new wife. Not your typical, young 'trophy wife,' but someone around his own age who looked good and must have been captivated by his charm and wealth. We were glad that he wouldn't be alone, because he was lost without my mother. It's weird to think how someone who forced his wife to kowtow to his needs couldn't live without a woman who was his, another of his possessions, but maybe that's exactly the crux," she added thoughtfully, "because it's precisely how his power manifests."

"I don't know much about my father's new partner. She's pleasant to us, and is wise enough to give us our space. Perhaps the wealth she enjoys is sufficient for her. Since my brother and I certainly have enough, we aren't envious of what he gives her."

"Anyhow, making a conscious decision, I chose not to share with my husband anything of what I'm going through. My friends cover for me when I'm at therapy. I continue acting as usual, and the only change is that I'm home a lot more with my children and less focused on myself. Of course, my kids are extremely happy about this. Suddenly I see how much they needed their mother's closeness: a caress, listening to them.

"For me, these past few months have also been a time of amazing discoveries. I could feel myself being more open to the next stage. That's when I started looking into courses and seminars, but secretly of course, covering up by saying I was looking for activities on art and enrichment. I can't say what drew me here when so many options are available. I hadn't even met with Avraham, only spoken to him by phone, but he reassured me that if I didn't wish to continue, I shouldn't feel obligated.

"So I started coming. And I apologize from the depth of my heart to each of you for coming late, for being impatient, for interrupting when people were talking by offering stupid comments, all of which were aimed at concealing my true self. I apologize for the dark glasses. I don't even know on which chapter of the book to focus my attention. Every chapter I read relates to something about me, about the life I created for myself, but now I see that I lack self-trust. I perceive myself as lacking worth.

"I use bright, outlandish clothes to say, 'Hey, look at my clothing but not at me, don't expect to see beyond them.' That's because beyond them is Sharon, not Shereene. Beyond the clothes is a woman who should have been independently successful, who would stand up for herself, who could have set her life path any way she wished, but gave her inner self away as a gift to a tyrant like a sacrifice offered on the altar of prosperity.

"Maybe now, after sharing everything with you, I can relate to the idea of being grateful to the Shekhinah for gifts I've been given. I can humbly say thank you for my accomplishments, which are much greater than I'd ever imagined. As the book says, 'Today in gratitude we lift our hearts above despair, and raise our thankful eyes, no longer looking downward to the dust.' That's it. I'm done," she smiled warmly, "and I've decided to turn the page. After the Passover meal, I'm planning on speaking to my husband.

"I've already prepared divorce papers with the lawyer. I've secretly opened my own bank account, and it made me so closely identify with your story, Sarai, and yours too, Eva, and that feeling of seeing your own name on the checks and the account. I hope to get your input on that, Sarai. I've consistently been depositing the cash my husband assumes is being used as spending money and, because he reckons I spend a lot, I've managed to put quite a tidy amount away. I didn't have my own credit card anyhow, so if he blocks me from accessing his accounts it's not going to make any difference.

"But I'm ready, and even looking forward to, living a less flashy life in favor of one with true content and happiness. I'm sure my father will help me financially. I might even try to see if he'll admit to his similar behavior toward my mother. He's softened with age, and he loves my children and my brother's children. My brother took over management of the manufacturing plant that's doing very well and of which I also have a share. I'm confident that if I tell my father I'm divorcing, he'll transfer my share of the company dividends to my account and not to the supposedly mutual account with my husband.

"Lastly, my dream is to utilize my knowledge in fashion, art and history, all of which I love, in some way. Maybe a satisfying idea will come of my wanderings through Europe's various markets over the years."

Shereene stopped speaking and gestured to show she'd finished her story. Group members reassured her that they'd support her as she set out on a new journey, and that she should feel free to phone them if she needed some advice or emotional support after confronting her husband. On one hand, she appeared vulnerable and confused, yet simultaneously galvanized and certain. To the group it felt as though a genie had burst out of its bottle but no one believed, right then, that she'd achieve a complete turn-around in her life before the yearlong course was complete.

Several months after the course had ended Eva, looking for a dinner service, walked into a store offering vintage art deco and art nouveau items. She knew exactly what she was after: large colorful plates with a style of design that was popular in the 1920s and 1930s and plain plates with a fine gold edging. Eva was greeted by a charming woman with straight brunette hair, attractive framed glasses, and black pants that showed off her fabulous body. Gazing more intensely into the woman's eyes, the two instantly recognized each other. Shereene! In smart sports shoes, and glasses 'for real this time,' she laughed.

They hugged each other warmly, happy to be meeting again.

"After the divorce which, you may remember from what I shared at the meetings, wasn't easy, I was so grateful for everyone's support that I decided to part from all my friends and acquaintances who called me 'Shereene' and move to a spacious, comfortable apartment with my children.

"My Dad was crestfallen, having finally understood what he caused my mother. He left his partner, lives alone, and devotes all his time to golf and the grandkids. I'm on good terms with my ex, who now has a very wealthy American girlfriend. But they don't live in the same home. My friends said she made it clear to him, in no uncertain terms, that she absolutely would not be dependent on any man. Maybe that's the best option for him, after the divorce. But one of the things that I did almost straight away was to begin learning about professional collecting. I decided to specialize in the areas I truly love: avant-garde fashion and art." She beamed at Eva. "And look! Here you are in my sanctuary!"

Eva chose a stunning set, to which Sharon added a beautiful Versace vase in gratitude for what they'd shared. That evening Eva hosted her family, the new dishes laid out on a black, embroidered tablecloth along with the new vase filled with red dahlias and sprigs from the garden's lemon tree. When her family walked in, they stopped in their tracks, saying it was one of the most beautiful tables they'd ever seen her set.

"At the end of our meal I'll tell you the story behind these plates," she promised them, smiling to herself.

CHAPTER 15

"Miracles are seen in light, and light and strength are one."

After the meeting that should have been the last before the Passover holiday hiatus, Avraham sent a group message requesting one more meeting before the break. He promised it'd be brief, but stressed that it was important, a kind of mid-term summary of materials learned so far.

Eva found she had little patience for his request. In a few days, her son would be marrying and she was excited, but also deeply sorrowful over the fact that she would not be there as part of a couple as she'd always hoped. She would arrive on her own, he would arrive on his own, and they would conduct themselves as two separate entities. Only the closest family and a handful of friends knew that any togetherness that might be displayed was nothing but show. It made the whole situation so much tougher for her, causing countless nights of tears and sleep-disrupting gut churning.

As always, Avraham sat facing and scanning them. This time Sharon was not only on time but arrived in advance, smiling, without her dark glasses. She took her hat off and put it on a chair to the side. Avraham smiled and asked everyone to say one word that expresses how they felt right then. Each answered: fear, uncertainty, admiration, acceptance, gratitude, collapse, connection, understanding. Eva shared that she was terribly excited but simultaneously fearful as the wedding was soon approaching.

Avraham added the word 'release.' Eva thought that was a bit strange: what did Avraham's choice of word imply? Despite the degree of openness they shared, there must clearly be a long way still to go to feel release from the obstacles in the relationship between mentor and mentees. But she decided to just let it ride.

"I'm extremely proud of each of you for how far you've come," Avraham opened the session, "for sharing your moving life stories, although Eva, even though she was the first to agree to speak, still hasn't fully shared her story and we've mostly only received hints through the stories of the rest of you. So perhaps," he added thoughtfully, turning to face her, "that was meant to be part of your journey too."

"But I want to tell you," Avraham continued, looking once again around to each member of the group, "that in the coming month and a half I won't be with you." Audible in-breaths of shock could be heard around the room. "An offer was presented to record 'A Course in Miracles' in Hebrew at an American studio. It's a significant step for the course and people interested in learning it. It will enable slipping the disc into the DV player on the home computer or in the car and listening to me read the book."

Indeed, thought Eva, that would be wonderful

"But I'm not leaving you unattended," Avraham reassured. "My amazing colleague, Efrat, will take my place. When you return after the Passover break, she'll mentor you in her unique way until I'm back."

Eva was angry and disappointed. Why now, when at last she was beginning to feel that what she was experiencing through the course was being effected into the positive change she wanted so badly?

"Well, I'm flying to the States anyhow, to see my daughter,

son-in-law and grandchildren, and then there's the wedding," she said to Avraham, "so I'm planning on waiting for you until you're back."

She could hear the undertone of anger as she spoke, and didn't understand why she even felt that way. Could it be because she was advancing to a state where she could step away from her marriage, from the pain that had been her close companion for the past thirty months, from everything familiar collapsing not just around her but around her children too? Her daughter, unable to watch her mother immersed in such deep pain on a daily basis, had moved to the US with the children. Everything was coming apart at the seams.

And to make things worse, just when she was taking real steps towards healing, Avraham was leaving? She knew Efrat was a very spiritual person, but someone more down to earth and intellectual like Avraham was better suited to Eva's personality when it came to the course materials.

"Sometimes a switch in mentor is exactly what's needed," Avraham said, nodding and smiling at her without adding anything further.

Avraham began the pre-break meditation, everyone linking arms in a great embrace before saying au revoir, until we meet again.

Eva's son and fiancé, who were living in Eva's home, were in a state of nervous excitement. Eva accompanied her future daughter-in-law to the bridal gown's first fitting: the young woman looked angelic. Eva flew to spend a week in America with her daughter, buying herself a dress for the wedding: black, with some sheer sections and lined in deep crimson. It suited her figure well, sported a deep neckline, and made Eva feel very feminine, especially once she slipped on her matching stilettos.

The wedding was a very happy affair. For the first time in her life, Eva danced with whomever she wished, joined in the circles of dancers, danced alone or with friends. It really was a joyful release, not feeling restricted by her husband's contemptuous expressions. Secretly she still held out hope that he'd invite her for the last waltz, but he never rose from his chair. Clearly no invitation was forthcoming.

Eva hadn't known how to dance but her husband, an excellent dancer, had taught her. She always felt so confident in his arms and the way he led. As the wedding approached, she couldn't imagine dancing with any other partner, but those thoughts led her to an interesting decision. Two months before the wedding she registered for a ballroom dancing course simply to see if she could handle being led by a different man.

And indeed, it was challenging. Her palms constantly sweated, which made her embarrassed. The teacher, noticing, decided to dance only with her during class until Eva slowly gained confidence, even doing 'the twist' which, until now, had been taboo from her husband's perspective. When he had danced it, his movements were so smooth and elegant that she'd simply sat at the sidelines watching and noticing how other women were rapt at his skill. But from the moment she let all that go, everything looked different. She'd never be an amazing dancer, but her enjoyment of dancing began to grow, and no less importantly, her embarrassment diminished in leaps and bounds.

The event was a sheer delight and the young couple was thrilled. Eva watched them: a lovely pair whose shared life was off to a great beginning, the entire family joining in their joyful occasion, her youngest grandchildren serving as flower girls. She watched the marriage taking place beneath the bridal canopy and felt euphoric. Right then she so badly wanted to take her husband's hand in her own: after thirty years together, shouldn't they enjoy their children's and grandchildren's happiest moments together?

As the wedding drew to a close, Eva felt tipsy with energy even though she'd hadn't even had as much as a sip of wine.

Leaving the hall, she made her way to her car. That's when the solitude hit her. Instead of excitedly recalling all the special moments together on the ride home, each of her son's parents got into their separate cars after no more than a polite peck on the cheek. Eva knew where her husband was headed: and it cut like a knife.

Back home, she studied herself once again in the mirror as tears rolled down her cheeks and her delicate makeup began to streak. But, for the first time in ages, she knew she not only looked well put together, but really great. It was an excellent way to start the next part of her journey.

It had been clear to her for a while that right after her son's wedding the divorce would be next on the agenda, but for now she deflected the thought.

She also realized that the day may come when a new man would enter her life. That led her to a decision that might have been seen as crazy, and perhaps charged by the energy from the wedding.

The biggest hurdle after thirty years of making love to one man was the thought of being naked with, or even kissing and embracing, another. These thoughts frightened her. She'd met a good-looking man at a café, and then again for a second time, following which he suggested they meet in his apartment. Eva knew exactly what she was getting herself into but decided to jump in with both feet and get beyond her fears.

Their love making was considerate, pleasant, and they parted ways. Eva knew she wouldn't be seeing him again. For her he was no more than a stepping stone along the way. She pulled up in her driveway but couldn't get out of the car: she was suddenly shocked by what she'd done and burst into hysterical sobs. Years of faithful marriage, on her part, had led to this moment of meaninglessness. It was simultaneously a turning point and a source of bitterness and disappointment.

She turned the music up loud but still couldn't pull herself together, and remained glued to the driver's seat bawling her eyes out. Suddenly her phone rang. She didn't answer even though she saw it was her daughter, probably wanting to know if she was alright. But the strident ring had jolted her sufficiently to get out of the car and go inside.

"I managed to do it but I'm so angry, so ashamed, so humiliated," she texted her friend, who'd encouraged her to go all the way. Not expecting any answer because it was so late, Eva realized that she was nevertheless feeling calmer for just having gotten that off her chest. She made a glass of cinnamon tea, poured half a shot glass of sherry into it, and called her daughter back.

"What's going on, Mom?" her daughter asked, sensing something was amiss.

"Everything's fine. I'm just super tired," Eva reassured.

CHAPTER 16

"Salvation comes from my one Self."

Meetings were resuming, this time with Efrat at the helm. Eva still strongly opposed the change of facilitator but, after what Avraham said, she decided to give things a chance and join in. Group members sat tensely, in anticipation, some feeling a lot better for the break, some feeling low and not knowing where they were heading just yet. Eva realized that she wasn't the only one experiencing difficulty with Avraham not being there to guide the sessions.

And then... the door swung open and an angel stood framed in the room's entrance. For Eva, no other words could describe that instant. A beautiful woman with bright eyes, blond hair, in a loose white tunic and filmy white shawl tossed over her shoulders with elegant abandon. Efrat Sar-Shalom smiled and, in a soft voice very dissimilar the tone used by Avraham which occasionally tended to be loud, began speaking:

"I understand the challenge you are all facing with Avraham being away for a while, but I promise that this temporary change will only be to your benefit," she began, after which she briefly spoke about herself, about being Avraham's student, about the journey that the course took her on, and the connection between herself and the desert.

"Ever since I was a child, I could sense a divine spirit watching over me. I had a connection with God that I couldn't explain," she began. Right away Eva began to relax, her resistance to Efrat evaporating as she experienced similar inexplicable senses of connection in her own life.

"At nine years old, I vowed to God that I would try to heal people, to bring harmony to our nation and to our people scattered worldwide, peace to the world, peace to the creatures of the sea, the land and plant life."

Efrat now sat down, took a few calming breaths, and continued. "I came across 'A Course in Miracles' through Dr. Phyllis Schlemmer, the healer and medium through which the material was attained, and who also authored 'The Only Planet of Choice,' an international bestseller." Eva recalled having read the book years earlier, before even hearing about the course, and being impressed by the book. She realized now that Avraham knew full well that Eva would connect instantly to Efrat as mentor.

"Phyllis suggested that several of my friends and other people she knew study the course material. I agreed immediately, and that's where Avraham and I met and our souls twinned. In that instant we, Avraham and I, realized that our souls were linked from other times. Once the course was over, I went my way, Avraham went his, and years later in a dire situation I joined the course again, led this time by Avraham. What I encountered there, this time around, was like nothing I'd ever been through before and, deep inside, it was clear to me that I needed to be alongside Avraham and teach this course.

"I was part of the team that helped Avraham translate the book. When he went to the States at some point to study transpersonal psychology and devote time to translating, I realized I'd be the one to carry on his work. As Avraham put it, 'someone has to preserve the eternal flame.' So in 1989 I began teaching and, since then, have been busy leading the course and spreading its message. From the moment Avraham and

I connected, there hasn't been a day where we haven't talked, taught together, shared ideas, and felt blessed by our deep friendship."

Gazing into Efrat's penetrating but compassionate eyes, listening closely to her tone and words, taking in the way she looked, and linking to her energy, completely captivated Eva.

Meetings with Efrat had a much more spiritual essence. For the most part, they went over materials already learned, practiced the exercises and focused on lessons dealing with several specific statements: 'Miracles are seen in light,' 'I am as God created me,' and 'Salvation comes from my one Self.'

It was markedly evident that the group members had slowly begun to connect more easily with, and practice, these statements. Each of them was on a path of healing, although forgiveness was still one of the most difficult and painful aspects for them all.

But they could all see the light at the end of the tunnel, and their manner at the meetings was already much gentler: noise from neighbors annoyed them less, for example; contact with spouses hurt them a little less and enabled calmer external discussion now that the internal discourse was reconsolidating. Understanding that salvation comes from within themselves and that an effort must be made to reach that point, while being less immersed in accusatory stances relative to the past and more focused on the present and a warm, loving future, seemed much more accessible now, even if the concept hadn't yet found its place in their hearts.

Avraham had explained that there would come a stage where the intellect understands, but the body is still directed to a different way of seeing. Eva had begun rereading spiritually focused works by Deepak Chopra and others that she'd first read when she was much younger. She searched for these books eagerly. Having invested two years in East Asian studies, she was very open to the region's cultures: Buddhism, Hinduism,

Shintoism, and so on, fascinated by them. She was pleased to have seen how, over time, a connection to the spiritual was not just her area of interest but that her younger son was drawn to it too, and could easily become a healer. It meant she could share her feelings and experiences with him knowing that he accepted them.

Eva began meditating on a daily basis, realizing that a divine force had opened her eyes that fateful Friday morning. It was clear: everything had happened for her benefit, despite the whelming difficulty, the fall, the pain. She needed to shed and release much in her life, including the extra weight on her body, and in her heart. Knowing that a clear link exists between body and mind, she began fearing that the lump she could feel in her throat and which made swallowing hard would eventually turn from a psychological blockage to a true, somatic one.

She decided that change would have to happen, sooner rather than later. To that end, she began getting together more with friends, giving free rein to heart-to-heart conversations. It occurred to her that everyone had actually seen and known, but no one could pluck up the courage to speak out, or even put an anonymous note under her door. Understanding why, she forgave that, too.

From the stories that group members shared, and those she heard from other men and women who'd experienced crisis in their lives, the hardest part was admitting that they felt like failures, and seeking help. How many catastrophic situations could have been avoided, she thought, if people simply said those three vital words: "I need help." It could even be conveyed as "I can't carry this anymore on my own."

Eva shared her realization with the group: there are actually countless people around us willing and happy to help if we'd only ask them. Efrat, seated opposite Eva, gave her that angelic smile.

"That's the moment of Godliness within you," she said,

"that moment of recognition, of being one with the power that guards over you."

Efrat asked the group members to sit, or lie down, for the meditation session, whichever was more comfortable. She began speaking in a soft voice. Eva was finding it much easier to close her eyes and enter a relaxed state, but she didn't always hear the instructions as thoughts swirled in her mind.

Efrat asked them to pass through a gate opening in front of them. Help, thought Eva, sometimes comes in a physical form such as assisting someone to rise and flee in the wee hours of the night. Help could be financial, such as Sharon's friends provided until she could stand on her own two legs.

Sometimes, as in Nathan's story, help came in the form of a slim volume which Eva had read before passing it on to someone else she met in a different group setting held after her children's marriages. That group was recommended by Eva's psychologist and geared to supporting Eva before divorcing. It had more of an intellectual nature, providing a kind of balance to 'A Course in Miracles' and its more emotional or spiritual character.

After reading Nathan's book, the fellow to whom Eva had given it found the courage to confront his wife, and their marriage was saved. He then forward it on to another friend who was staving her children off from leaving the family home but couldn't see how her actions were impacting them. The book led her to realize that she was addicted to her own tribulations and, in turn, preventing her children from getting on with their own lives. No doubt, thought Eva, the book has gone on to others by now!

Furthermore, Eva thought, help is listening. Sometimes that's all a person needs in order for their life to be saved, as so frequently transpired on the night hotline. Too often people don't realize the incredible power that a kind word can have.

A single word. It can utterly deflate a person; it can encourage someone toward improvement. As effortlessly as Eva could say these words to others, she wasn't always willing to listen to the words she was told, to see the good, to understand that she actually is a strong woman and that she would, eventually, grow from all the challenges in her life, but those supportive phrases were slowly being internalized.

Morning conversations with her sister. Her sister's encouragement. Eva remembered how it sometimes angered her but, slowly, her sister's words penetrated heart and mind and provided Eva with a new perspective. When we're in a low place, Eva thought, we're sure we're the only ones going through tough times and, anyone who isn't, couldn't possibly understand us. And yet, Eva knew how valuable it had been to have her attentive sister always ready to listen, and to see that there really are good, supportive people around us who only wish to see us doing well.

"Now I want you to see yourselves in a hovering white bubble," Eva heard Efrat say, but Eva sank into another round of thoughts. If someone hurts you, it's not really meant at you but indicates their own state of vulnerability, even though that's difficult to see and accept. Eva was beginning to see that this was the way to forgiveness. One statement which helped her get through one day after the next was the fourth agreement in Ruiz's 'The Four Agreements.' It centered around doing one's best for that day, for that moment, and not agonizing over what else might have been possible but was missed or left undone.

The Tibetan gong sounded. Eva cleared her mind. She suddenly realized that she'd hardly noticed the time spent meditating. Efrat must surely have guided them through slowly waking, but Eva hadn't heard a word. She smiled: if she'd been so deeply immersed in meditation, it must be beneficial for her. Up until then she'd always been attentive to guided meditation and assisted by the instructions; suddenly now she could enter the meditative state on her own, clear her mind, and be in internal tranquility.

"I'm initiating a seminar inviting this group along with members of other groups that studied with Avraham and me. It'll be a weekend in the desert, at a wonderful location near Arad," Efrat said as the meeting came to an end. "Who's coming?"

Eva's hand was the first to go up. As with her virgin trip to India, she knew that places such as these, and encounters of these kinds, were the best for facing the unpredictable, the unexpected, taking another step on the journey. They were where she could find her other self: not the architectural planner and designer, but other parts of her being, that other voice that had a burning desire to help. Perhaps that's where the first seed on becoming a group facilitator was sown. For good reason, it seemed, Avraham had said she should be in his chair.

CHAPTER 17

"Light and joy and peace abide in me."

Along the way, Eva picked up two friends from the group for the drive south to Arad. Even when she was with her own family, Eva always preferred to be in the driver's seat, trusting her own driving skills. The time passed in pleasant conversation against a background of classical music. At last she found the signpost to turn off the main road onto a path that led deep into the desert. Teepees provided the sleeping arrangements and surrounded a circular structure where meetings would be held. Each teepee came equipped with a radiator to ward off the desert's chilly nights.

After setting themselves up in their tents, people gathered in the round room and the program began. A large number of students had come for this weekend, which was an opportunity to meet interesting people who'd already altered their life trajectories, from a change of career to better parenting or regaining closeness within the family, and so on.

The weekend offered an array of interesting lectures: mysticism, astronomy, the healing power of the moment and, of course, several types of meditation sessions.

Welcoming the Sabbath on Friday evening was very spiritual, marked by great respect for the Creator and the world. It was a quiet moment in the desert darkness dotted by countless sparkling stars, as though the infinite enveloped those present, imbuing them with a feeling of sanctity.

After lunch on Saturday, Efrat asked each of the attendees to spend time on their own in the sweeping expanse of the desert. "Try to home in on what you want in your life," she said. "Try to feel the infinite in this vastness."

Eva wandered off until she found a cliff overlooking an abyss. Having suffered acrophobia ever since her daughter was born, a fear that grew with each childbirth, she sat at the top of the rock, closed her eyes, and tears unexpectedly rolled down her cheeks. Realizing she was gripping the rock with all her strength, she opened her hands and eyes, and noticed an eagle with massive wings catching the breeze and gliding along the dry wadi deep in the valley below. How she envied that eagle. She trembled in a moment of fear, but soon felt how she could be merging with the cosmos. Remembering the tumultuous moment when she'd parked on the seafront and the accompanying sense of helplessness at that time, her fears resurfaced.

In her mind she replayed her recent intimate encounter, followed by a sense of betrayal. How could her husband have come home day after day following intimate relations with other women, only to conduct himself with her and their family as though nothing had happened? He had hugged her, kissed her, they had been the perfect couple: so how could he have led this double life? Or perhaps I'm being self-righteous, Eva wondered. Maybe it's just human nature and perhaps, as a friend had suggested, it had been instructive in making their lives seem perfectly balanced? She didn't know what to think.

A murder of squawking crows streaked across the sky, breaking Eva's chain of thoughts. Gathering small stones around her, she shaped a kind of marker, stone balanced on stone like an ancient burial site, as though putting to rest what had shocked her so deeply. It connected with the day she'd driven to the beachfront and burned all the letters, notes, and cards she'd written to her husband over the years. She knew both actions were merely symbolic, and wasn't sure they would bring long-lasting salvation, but she did feel that concealed threads drawing her into the abyss were weakening. She spread her arms, mimicking the eagle, and screamed until her voice mingled with the crows' shrieks.

"I'm letting go! I'm releasing myself from the chains of prohibitions, from the shackles of poor self-esteem I've lived with for years, from the manacles of knowing and fear of the unknown, from clinging to what was!"

It was the most freeing sensation Eva had ever experienced. She collected a few more stones and put them in her bag to remind her of this moment. Gazing at the marker she'd built, she hoped it would remain there forever as a sign that she'd been there but hadn't given up.

As she walked back to the round room, she saw Efrat coming her way, smiling, her arms held out.

"We all heard your scream!" she said, "and knew it was the good kind."

The weekend ended with a meditation focused on gratitude for the place, the space, and the self.

Driving back with her friends, the air was charged. Classical music played in the background all the way, making it easier for them to remain silent, introspective.

CHAPTER 18

"Into His Presence would I enter now."

Avraham was back the following week. As usual, he gazed at each of the group's members, and sighed in deep gratitude as he smiled at Eva.

"So sometimes it's necessary?" he asked.

"Yes," she answered, smiling.

"Your auras are wonderfully and colorfully lit. Something in you is aglow today. Let's sit in a circle and begin, this time without meditation."

Eva asked if she could read the statements she'd marked before the meeting. She particularly connected with 'This day is holy [...] You have spent long days and nights in celebrating death. Today you learn to feel the joy of life.'

"I understand that, from here on, all the doors reopen," she shared, "and that I can begin taking a path I'd never dreamt of realizing. As the book says, I allowed the Shekhinah out there in the desert to dream of the journey I start today, for me. Yesterday my husband phoned and asked to talk with me. I knew what the conversation would be about. He asked to realize the divorce agreement we drew up some nine months earlier. It was signed but hadn't been ratified, nor had we opened a file for the divorce procedure.

"On one hand I was crushed. On the other hand, I understood

that it couldn't be any other way, with the difficult thoughts on an endless loop. For months, my husband kept breaking one promise after another to leave the other woman and free himself of the relationship, not meet with her and give us a chance. I came to the conclusion that I can't continue living with this chasm. We decided it was best to split. In a month from today we will sign the bill of divorce."

Eva's voice broke. She sobbed, but it was a different kind of crying, not one of terrible pain but of a mix of release and fear over the unknown. "And so I see that the next chapter of my life begins now. I can even forgive, because I really can see that these events took place not because of me, but to me."

"I read in the next chapter that the time when my doubts will cease has already been determined, and that now I need to say thanks for this place in my life and carry on, grateful for the painful period. I see that Chapter 59 talks of acknowledging miracles I've received. By virtue of the blessings and goodness I've received in my life, I can give gifts to the cosmos and not just experience them myself," Eva continued. "All I want to do now is visit my parents to thank them for bringing me into this world, thank them for their humanity and kindness.

"I want to tell you a little about that so you can follow what I'm about to tell you and where I'm coming from. My parents' home and their furniture store were an open house for anyone who came along. People knew they could come into the shop on a cold day and receive a hot drink, an item of clothing, a blanket, or just warm themselves by the fire. On a hot day they could enjoy the fan's breeze, later replaced by the air conditioner. At any time at all, they could sit and chat, receive an encouraging, kind word and sometimes, secretly, money would slip into their pocket. My parents weren't just a home for my sister and me, but also for friends who knew that they could talk about anything, lighten their load, and my parents would be there to listen and give them a supportive hug.

"These were the years right after the Second World War, and most of the families my parents knew were survivors of Europe's concentration camps. Very few survivors had grandparents, parents, or even siblings. These friends were our surrogate families. That's how a really distant cousin would suddenly be treated as immediate family. My parents' home, small as it was, somehow always managed to hold more and more people. There was also an openness towards talking about the Holocaust in ways that were taboo in other homes. My school friends even enjoyed ice cream in winter, a no-no in their own homes, as my sister and I were always allowed it at our home.

"We grew up with this tremendous sense of tolerance and love towards everyone, other than perhaps the Hungarians and the Nazis that my father could never forgive. But even in that regard a change occurred when two mixed couples from Germany showed up. The wives were German, not Jewish, if I remember rightly. Perhaps that's when my parents reached a state of forgiveness.

"Nor can I ever thank them enough for their help with my children all these years. They were a source of strength for me and for my children, who are very attached to them. They protected them. They made sure the children had what they needed in just the same way they looked after me and my sister when we were little girls, but they were also able to step aside when appropriate.

"As teens, my sister and I were the first among our friends to receive our driving licenses because, as my mother said, 'women need to be independent.' My mother also drove, and although most of her friends didn't work, my mother managed the shop profitably, drove the van and was a trail-blazer in many ways.

"She also directed us, gently, saying that a woman must have a profession. Perhaps that was to compensate for her own adolescence, spent in Auschwitz and other labor camps, which prevented her from realizing her own dream of being an x-ray technician in the hospital where her father worked as an accountant.

"After she came here, she immediately enlisted with the Haganah, which later became the Israel Defense Forces. She wanted to be useful in protecting her country and people. She met my father when visiting the home of her great-grandmother who lived in Jerusalem. In fact, my parents are distant cousins, two wonderful, talented people who love each other very much, but who also argue with each other over everything.

"But make no mistake: we had a very happy childhood. I didn't stand out in school, at least until high school. I was transparent. When I was fifteen, a grandfather who lived in America and was a pulpit rabbi sent boat tickets for my mother and we girls to visit him. Perhaps that's where my cosmopolitan side was born, and the idea that we're part of a bigger world and, even if it conducted itself evilly towards my parents and my people to a degree that the mind cannot fathom, there's still an entire massive world out there to discover and learn about. It was a time when kids didn't really go on trips abroad, and certainly not so far away.

"Starting high school also opened up a new place for me in the world, where the adolescent no longer hides, isn't transparent anymore but seen. My confidence radiated when walking down the street in the most current fashions with super-mini-skirts that my mother actually sewed for me. Even in tough times, we didn't feel them so much because our mother made us the most amazing outfits using the best and most interesting furnishing fabrics and in the latest styles.

"I loved being in my parents' shop. They also made the furniture they sold, my mother did the upholstery, and I loved advising clients about color matching. That's when I decided to study architecture and design.

"Before I enlisted for my military service, a cousin from

Brazil sent me a ticket to visit him in Sao Paulo. Thinking back, I'm so grateful to my parents for their trust which, even today, can't be taken for granted. They knew I would manage just fine, even if the flights were long, involving stopovers, connecting flights, and a foreign language. It took almost two days to get there, which is when I called to tell them I'd arrived okay, and described how my cousin had waited for me on the tarmac next to the plane's stairs, orchids in his hands.

"Brazil is where I discovered my independence and ability to make my way in the big wide world. I also experienced sexual harassment by one of the embassy staff but, luckily for me, I was sufficiently assertive to deflect him and push the whole incident out of my mind. It occurred to me, though, that it was an experience that seemed to declare: 'Welcome to the real world, where men think they can do whatever they want and where women are an object or game for their pleasure.' That's when my mother's warning about male attackers suddenly clicked. She even taught us how fight back, which was very helpful."

"Since I already had my driver's license before enlisting, and the army was opening up what were considered male positions to women, I decided to be a driver. Of course in the armored unit I was sent to, no commander agreed to have a woman as his personal driver so I ended up at a desk job. That's where I met Aliza, my best friend to this day, even with the occasional lapses in keeping connected.

"I wasn't happy in a clerical job. Eventually I was transferred to a different unit where I officially became the IDF's first woman driver. It's also where I met my first husband, an air force commander, a real hunk, a charmer. We married about a week after I finished my military service. Then I registered for architecture studies at Haifa's Technion, and bible studies in Haifa University, but my husband wasn't agreeable to me taking on a five-year study program, so I forewent my plan for the sake of a compromise on night classes in architectural planning and design at the Technion. I capitulated to the dictates of the time, but I think it was the last time in my life that I did.

"Nine months later my daughter was born. 'A girl giving birth to a girl,' family and friends said, laughing. I resumed my studies. My parents offered a lot of support. Then the Yom Kippur War broke out. My father, a military paramedic, was recruited to the Sinai area, my sister had a full-time military career anyway, and my mother and I were left alone with the baby. And that's when I began seeing that perhaps marrying had been a mistake, that perhaps I'd gone into it too quickly and it wasn't the best choice for me personally, that I wanted more from life.

"I couldn't have pinpointed what 'more' implied, but something was burning and churning inside me. I waited until my father was back home from the war, safe and sound, and we were standing in their kitchen when I told my husband that I want to divorce. I honestly don't remember his reaction! But my parents supported my decision, respecting my considerations even though it was socially very unacceptable at the time.

"That's how a new trajectory took shape. I completed my studies, which brought me into contact with a wide variety of men from classes and my day job. One night the doorbell rang. It was after midnight and a voice I recognized asked hesitantly, 'Are you awake?' I opened the door to the man who had been a childhood friend's husband. She was about two years younger than me and had passed away some months earlier, but we were very close and my parents were like the siblings her parents never had.

"From that moment on, a journey of love began, accompanied by countless questions and deliberations: what am I doing, and how would it affect my friend's parents, was it disrespectful towards their beloved daughter? I didn't want to hurt anyone.

"But life is a powerful force and a year later, he and I married. Not everything went smoothly with my parents' friends who were, in essence, my husband's parents, especially since unfounded rumors were flying around. Those rumors hurt us deeply, and also led to my parents cutting contact with my partner's parents, their closest friends. I never got angry, but I cried a good deal over that rift.

"Our first son was born on my deceased girlfriend's birthday. Maybe that softened them because every year, when my husband visited them, they always sent back a gift for me as well as for our two additional sons, but especially for my daughter, who they loved so much and who, for them, was like a granddaughter.

"Then routine took over. A good life based on love. That was my experience. Both of us were self-employed and doing well. We built a beautiful, spacious semi-detached home together with another family, good friends. We raised wonderful children, assisted by my parents who were always there for us. I can't say if there were cracks in the relationship but I, at least, didn't feel any. From my perspective, my children's father was my best friend, my confidante, my supporter, and so proud of me and my achievements.

"That's why, on that bitter morning when I allowed myself to truly open my eyes, the crisis I experienced was so intense. Realizing that I'd been living with someone who didn't really love me, who loved other women, who took advantage of my absolute trust in him, left me shocked and in deep pain. I felt as though I was an actor in 'The Merchant of Venice' and that someone had just forcibly and mercilessly slashed off a pound of my flesh, ripped out a part of my body and my soul.

"I felt doubly betrayed by women I knew who, on one hand, were my friends but on the other, it turns out, were having affairs with my husband. The crisis hit me on two fronts simultaneously. And then there was the pain I felt relative to my parents, who love my husband like their own son."

Suddenly Eva went completely quiet. She hadn't even

noticed how long she'd been talking. She didn't look at anyone, as though having an out-loud discussion with herself. An uncomfortable silence filled the room. Eva slowly raised her head and saw tears in everyone's eyes. It seemed that everyone had reacted emotionally at the same moment. Each of the group member's had withdrawn into their own being and sorrowful events.

Spontaneously they drew their chairs closer to each other, creating a closed, tight circle which included Avraham. Spontaneously, they reached out, seeking each other's hands and began to sing Adit Pank's "The Days Ahead," as though the song had become the group's anthem. Spontaneously, everyone stood, and remained standing in their places in the circle, linking arms, swaying as they sang, each of them immersed in her or his thoughts.

It was a moment of comprehension: sharing their stories was the most powerful aspect of their healing. Now they could see how healing was indeed within themselves, and that only they could differentiate between their own light and darkness and surface from their own story, even if it needed some time to take shape and come into the open. They realized that they are, as they'd read, the sum of their own thoughts.

Eva remembered a statement from the book, picked it up, found the place, and asked to read it aloud. "Thoughts are not big or little, powerful or weak. They are merely true or false. Those that are true create their own likeness. Those that are false make theirs."

They remained standing in a circle until slowly the circle began to drift apart and people began collecting their belongings, saying goodbyes, hugging each other. Over the remaining sessions, when they completed the book, each of them would learn more about themselves. By the year's end, each would have reached a better place in their lives.

Epilogue

As the course was coming to a close, Avraham told the group that he had been diagnosed with cancer. It was the most painful meeting of the year. Instantaneous, everyone put their own woes aside and concentrated on Avraham's difficulties and suffering, even though he remained hopeful.

The course concluded, but the group met several times with Avraham in his home. He was weak, but angelic Efrat was there for him, together with several of his friends, leading the course in his stead. Over time, the connections between the group's members waned, other than that of Eva and Emily. As Avraham had said: "You came together here for a specific purpose and for good reason your souls chose each other."

Eva's divorce proceedings were finalized and, in time, she met someone who became her new partner. He made her feel extremely feminine and constantly valued. That relationship also came to an end but, by then, Eva was already very aware of how things were developing and knowingly decided not to remain in a relationship she didn't feel was right for her. She sold her home and built a new house in the Golan Heights.

One day, during their trip to France, she and her partner of the time were touring the ancient, picturesque and walled town of Saint Paul. Eva's dog Shadow, now quite old, had remained with her daughter who had meanwhile returned to Israel with her husband and their three children. Eva's parents helped look after their grandchildren with care and love while Eva's daughter and husband continued developing their careers. The sky was a clear blue. Not a cloud marked it. Eva was about to get out of the car when a large black cloud scudded across the sky. At that very moment, her daughter texted her: "Shadow collapsed."

Eva burst into tears and begged her daughter to try and keep him going for another day until she could get the first flight back to part from him in person. As she cried, a heavy rain began to fall, and a second text message showed on her phone: "Avraham has just passed away."

Eva sat in the car, crying as hard as the raindrops crashing against the windshield.

Then the rain stopped as suddenly as it began. The next day Eva flew back home, taking her beloved pet to the vet, who put it down gently as Eva cradled her. Bending low over Shadow, she whispered in its ear: "Go to Avraham, who must be in that astral world where all is good, and bring him my love."

She stepped out of the clinic and returned home with mixed feelings of joy and sorrow. Sinking into a garden chair, she watched the sun set between the rooftops, coloring the sky in brilliant cerise and orange. Suddenly, through her tears, an insight flashed into her mind: she was ready for any journey, for whatever the future has in store: every hardship she'd experienced so far had truly turned out to be a life lesson. Her four children, she knew, would always be anchors, along with her son-in-law, daughters-in-law, and her nine angelic grandchildren.

Just then a white butterfly flew by. Eva remembered her mother's words. "When I was a child my mother, Naomi, said that when a butterfly appears in front of you, it's a loving soul that has come to convey its love."

Ever since, even after her parents passed away, whenever Eva sat in the garden of whichever home she was living and a butterfly flew by, Eva would greet it with "Hi, Nana, hi Papa," and smile.

Eva went on to receive certification in group facilitation from the renowned Wingate Academic Institute. Some of the eleven women participating in that course became close friends. Focusing on supporting women experiencing complex challenges, Eva would begin by placing the stones she'd collected in the desert on the table. They served as a reminder of her journey of alignment with her own destiny, a testament that people do have the power to heal themselves, and they represented her gratitude for the blessings and miracles throughout her journey.

Is Eva's journey complete? No, it continues to bring her twists, turns and surprises; however, whenever she faces a hurdle, she envisions herself at the bottom of the stairs, confidently climbing upwards.

Exercise

Each and every one of you, in moments of crisis or hardship, must ask yourselves several questions.
If you were compelled by the processes the protagonists of this book went through, I recommend the following exercise you can each do on your own.

Ask yourselves:

1. What are the three things preventing me from attaining the future to which you currently aspire?
2. Of these three things, which do I think will create the biggest change in my life if I could resolve it?
3. What would my future look like if I resolved this issue?
4. Think of three actions I can take that would make my future better.
5. Think of one of those three actions and write it down, feel it vibrate inside me physically and emotionally.
6. Now write down what I can do today to achieve the future I wish for myself.

I would love to hear from you on my website:

thereeloflife.com

Acknowledgements

When I sat down to acknowledge all those who have been by my side, I realized that I could write another book just for this purpose.

Since my dark days, wonderful friendships have been rekindled and many new ones have been sparked, teaching me that lifelong friendships can be made at any age.

I would like to give a special thanks to:

The late *Avi Yasur*, who translated the book *Course in Miracles* to Hebrew with the help of others. He was the teacher of life, my mentor in a special year, who impacted my psyche forever. He is the inspiration for this book.

Efrat Sar Shalom, who has continued carrying the torch in Avi's footsteps. I met you in the desert, where you helped me decide to give a chance to a new future. Later, you gave me your blessing to rely on *Course in Miracles* for my book.

Dr. Iris Riches. You were my safety net and guiding hand when I stepped beyond fear into days of light.

Meirav Sever. For your attentiveness, astute words, and acupuncture care that hit all the right release points with precision.

My friends, for being there for me. Our friendships will burn forever.

Tali Teichman. We talk in the morning and again in the evening. What would I do without you?

Dita Liron. My neighbor who heard, saw, and gave me the first hug.

Limor Haim Matityahoo. You've taught me everything about marketing, AI, and more.

Avri Beeri, my partner. You were the first to read every chapter and encouraged me throughout.

Yehudit Gamadi; Nili Libovitsh; Aliza Porat; Sam Dahan; Noga Oppenheim; Raya Levanon; Haya Gal; Dalia Levy; Odeda Bar; Hana Fidelman; and Carmit Ben-David Albeck.

www.ingramcontent.com/pod-product-compliance
Lightning Source LLC
Chambersburg PA
CBHW071222230926
51849CB00001B/6